Praise for Tahmina Watson

Tahmina Watson's book establishes that despite the hopelessness that feels pervasive in America, there are those who continue to fight tirelessly to protect our rights, our children, our lands and those who are most vulnerable in today's America.

—Christine Berg, Former Mayor of Lafayette, Colorado

This book is a must read for fearless warriors, who sacrificed and have fought hard for justice. The author, Tahmina Watson, is a skilled and compassionate leader in the fight against injustice against immigrants in the Trump era. Her leadership has not only affected many vulnerable people, but she has organized the community in a powerful way. This book devotes chapters to the difference local attorneys and others, such as Bob Ferguson, Washington State's Attorney General, have made in the immigrant community. The examples in this book can be used on a national scale. Tahmina is able to brilliantly weave these stories into a strong community response to one of the most difficult times in history.

—Michele Carney, Carney & Marchi Law, Seattle, WA

Wars can make unlikely heroes, which is just what happened when Donald Trump declared war on asylum seekers and some brave lawyers stepped into the breach. Tahmina Watson masterfully recounts the heartbreaking, shameful and ultimately hopeful stories of this dark chapter in American history.

—Steve Leveen, author of *America's Bilingual Century*

Legal Heroes in the Trump Era is a book both hopeful and disturbing. Hopeful because we learn of a cadre of truly selfless defenders of the law and the pro bono work they have been doing—tirelessly and constantly—for immigrants since Trump took office. And disturbing because of how relentlessly and urgently these "immigrants' angels" are needed with Trump in charge. After reading Legal Heroes, I now understand that as the immigrants to America go, so go the citizens of America —we earlier immigrants. The absence of constitutional process that many immigrants now experience is a canary-in-the-coal-mine caution for all Americans of how vigilant we must be in protecting We, The People. No doubt every attorney will appreciate Legal Heroes, but even as someone not schooled in the law, I found the book a welcome reassurance that there are so many unsung heroes working to make this country unbroken.

—Mim Harrison author of *Smart Words: Vocabulary for the Erudite*

LEGAL HEROES IN THE TRUMP ERA

Be Inspired. Expand Your Impact. Change the World.

TAHMINA WATSON

Published by Watson Immigration Law

Seattle, Washington USA www.watsonimmigationlaw.com

ISBN: Print 978-1-7357585-0-3

ISBN: E-book 978-1-7357585-1-0

Alex Stonehill, Managing Editor

Caroline Doughty, Editor

Mim Harrison, Editor

Cover design by Raffy Ferras Hoylar

Author's photograph by Michael Doucett

Contents

For my daughters Sofia (10) and Sarina (8), my pride and joy. I hope this book will inspire you to make the world a better place.

And for Lornet Turnbull, my dear friend, editor, and a beloved journalist. You helped me learn that my knowledge and voice are important to share with the world. Forever grateful.

To the Memory of Justice Ruth Bader Ginsburg

Last year during the Thanksgiving holiday, my family and I drove through the deserted roads of Nevada under the bluest of skies to visit the Grand Canyon. As we drove, we listened to the entire audiobook, "Conversations with RBG" by Jeffrey Rosen. My husband Tom, who is also a lawyer, my daughters, and I were all in awe of her. The majesty of the Grand Canyon seemed to match the majesty that Justice Ginsburg brought to our world.

Justice Ginsburg died as I was finishing this book.

She has been an incredible inspiration to me, to all the lawyers highlighted in this book, and to countless others. Her tireless work defending and protecting women's rights, and the rights of the vulnerable was an inspiration even before she was seated at the US Supreme Court. And once there, her intellect and compassion for people shone through her numerous historic precedents and famous dissents which have touched the lives of virtually everyone in this country.

Justice Ginsburg demonstrated to us throughout her life that the law can be used as a tool to help the defenseless and shape society. We all must continue to work towards justice in her memory, just as she would have wanted, and not let all that she fought for to be in vain.

Thank you, Justice Ginsburg, for being the original Legal Hero, trailblazing the path for the rest of us.

Foreword

I was honored when Tahmina invited me to write the foreword for this book, which evolved from her podcast – *Tahmina Talks Immigration* – and, more specifically, her series entitled *Legal Heroes in the Trump Era*. I had the opportunity to be one of her guests in the series, and it was an engaging discussion.

When Tahmina told me she wanted to compile the *Legal Heroes* interviews into a book, I thought it was a great idea. She described her vision, and her hope that the book would serve as a call to action for the legal community to work together to confront injustice and inequality. As lawyers, we have the ability to bring about meaningful change, particularly during these difficult and unprecedented times. Tahmina is doing just that. She is a skilled attorney and passionate advocate for immigration reform. She has demonstrated fearless leadership and the ability to create new pathways to bring legal skills to the community.

Among these pages, you will hear from people who believe that our voices are powerful in igniting the change we want to see in this world. For example, Aneelah Afzali walked away from a lucrative career as a corporate lawyer to focus on community service. She has devoted her life to the fight for justice and equality.

Takao Yamada utilizes his talent and resources to connect technology entrepreneurship with activism to expand the social justice impact of both. He is also co-founder of Airport Lawyer, a team of individuals and organizations that helps vulnerable immigrant and refugee families in need of legal assistance.

And Joan Tierney decided to return to her roots as a pro bono lawyer after a decade as an Administrative Law Judge. After "retiring," she cut her teeth in immigration law by taking on a case involving a Honduran woman seeking asylum in the United States to escape domestic violence in her home country.

These and the other stories featured in this book inspire me to get out there and fight the good fight.

The dinner table discussions that my wife and I have with our young twins often remind me of what is at stake if we do not respond swiftly in the face of injustice. In these conversations, we talk about people in history who took action at great personal risk, and how their courage ultimately changed the world. This book provides us with many more examples of inspired leadership and positive role models that we look forward to sharing with them.

The law is a powerful tool to confront injustice. Everyone is accountable to the rule of law, including the president of the United States. Now is the time to be bold, and I share Tahmina's hope that this book will motivate others to get involved.

Bob Ferguson,
Washington State Attorney General
September 2020

Introduction

On Friday evening, January 27th, 2017, thousands of lawyers descended upon airports across the United States. It was a moment of profound realization for many. Lawyers would be needed like never before — throughout the Trump presidency — as officers of the court, protectors of the rule of law, and watchmen and women of democracy.

This book is a snapshot, and a sample of what a handful of legal heroes have accomplished in the last four years.

There isn't a civil or legal right that has not been violated by this administration. Trump and his administration have openly defied the Supreme Court in their actions on Deferred Action for Childhood Arrivals (DACA). Checks and balances are all but gone. And without them, the Constitution is but a document.

But lawyers are here to stay.

Personally, my concern for the sanctity of the law, rights, and liberties of all human beings has led me to step into a role in my community that didn't exist before.

In the absence of leadership, one must chart one's own path. All the lawyers in this book have done just that — whether it's to sue the administration when no one else would, or to build a grassroots network to pull together the nation's lawyers, or to write a play to educate the public about the opaque nature of immigration courts, especially as the erection of white tent immigration courts evokes the shameful memories of the Japanese Incarceration.

There are many lawyers around the country who have been doing incredibly profound work over the last four years. The profiles in this book are mostly people whose work I've seen up close. It derives from a series for my podcast *Tahmina Talks Immigration* called Legal Heroes in the Trump Era.

The Washington State Attorney General **Bob Ferguson** was the first AG to file a lawsuit against Trump, immediately upon the implementation of the first travel ban. Since then, there have been many more. But it's important to remember the immense bravery and courage it took to be the first to sue a brand-new president and win. Ferguson and his team set the standard for the fights that were to follow.

The American Civil Liberties Union (ACLU) has been an ardent defender of civil rights throughout the decades. But it has played a particularly incredible role since January 2017. **Michele Storms**, the executive director of the Washington state chapter of ACLU, left a comfortable job to take leadership of the ACLU WA just as Trump came into office. She probably hasn't slept properly since, leading various civil rights challenges including immigration, Black Lives Matter, and more.

As I was in the process of creating the Response Committee of the Washington Chapter of the American Immigration Lawyers Association, to ensure I could lead the efforts of immigration lawyers locally, someone else was doing the same down in Atlanta. Except she was preparing to lead lawyers from across the entire country. **Traci Feit Love** recognized that all civil rights would be under attack soon, and that lawyers would be necessary at every step. She founded Lawyers for Good Government, and has been leading the charge on almost every major legal issue that has arisen since.

Climate change is one of the most important issues of our

time. It is important not just for our children's future, but for the very existence of the world. And American climate policy leads the way for the global environment. **Drew Caputo**, Vice President for Litigation for Lands, Wildlife, and Oceans at Earthjustice, recognized that Trump would attack our environmental protections. So he and his team took prompt measures, and have been on the front lines on legal efforts to address climate change.

Aneelah Afzali was a corporate lawyer in private practice until a little before the 2016 election. She founded MAPS AMEN, the advocacy arm of the Muslim Association of Puget Sound, recognizing that Trump's campaign rhetoric was signaling rising Islamophobia that would only get worse once he was in office. Sure enough, he kept true to his campaign promise of a "Muslim Ban" as best he could. Afzali has used her legal background and her network to bring together the greater community in Seattle and afar to advocate against Islamophobia.

Erin Albanese is a force of nature. She sees a problem and she dives in to help. As a corporate lawyer specializing in business and nonprofit law, she has helped many advocacy organizations get off the ground. She was one of the few people who instantly recognized the vision I had for WIDEN and rolled her sleeves up to help make it a reality. But she didn't stop there. She co-founded Lawyer Moms of America in mid-2018 and has grown it to almost 15,000 members. From flying immigrants around the country to writing letters to congressional representatives, to fundraising for key causes, she's put her mark on the world.

I first met **Takao Yamada** within a couple days of the first travel ban going into effect. He was one of the first lawyers to show up at Sea-Tac Airport to help, as a volunteer with the International Rescue Committee. We were two of the five co-founders of Airport Lawyer in February 2017, which became a critical platform for connecting distressed passengers to volunteer lawyers during those historically chaotic times. Takao has since helped me co-found WIDEN as well.

Diversity education has never been more important in America. The recent Black Lives Matter protests following the death of George Floyd highlight that institutional racism must be confronted head-on. One way is to educate our children, the next generation of Americans. **Fiona McEntee** is a nationally acclaimed immigration lawyer who has been at the forefront of fighting unjust and discriminatory immigration policies. As a mother of two, she recognizes the transformative potential of the values children internalize. So she wrote a children's book celebrating the immigrant experience.

Margaret O'Donnell is another accomplished immigration lawyer who tapped into the power of storytelling to further the cause of immigrant rights. She realized that people didn't really understand what happens inside an immigration court, many of which are closed to the public. The human impacts of increased detention and deportation and tent courts on the southern border aren't easy to fathom based on statistics and headlines alone. So, she created a unique and interactive theatrical production called "The Detention Lottery" to put audiences eye-to-eye with the injustice hidden from view.

Shelly Garzon is an award-winning, nationally renowned medical malpractice lawyer, and partner at FAVROS Law in Tacoma, Washington. She was one of our first cohorts for WIDEN. Shelly is an exemplary, compassionate, and hard-working lawyer. She has taken multiple cases from WIDEN even though her own caseload is grueling. Knowing and experiencing firsthand that detained immigrants have no chance without a lawyer, she steps up over and over again. Her motto of "just do it" is an inspiration to all.

Jill Scott is the Director of Legal at a biotech company. She too is from the first cohort of the WIDEN cases. Like Shelly, she didn't stop at taking on just one case. In fact, she took her passion for justice all the way to the US-Mexico border to help destitute asylum seekers.

Matt Adams is the legal director at the Northwest Immigrant

Rights Project. His federal litigation practice has grown over decades. But no period has been more important than these last few years. His winning litigation strategies and precedent-setting cases in the Trump era have enabled lawyers around the country to protect their individual clients.

And finally, I met **Joan Tierney** over a decade ago when we were both serving on the board of Washington Women Lawyers. She was an Administrative Law Judge at the time. She retired in 2017, but it hasn't slowed her down at all. Quite the opposite — in retirement, she's found the freedom to do pro bono work to her heart's content, including as a volunteer with WIDEN. Every day she challenges herself to take at least one action to advance access to justice. She is a wife, mother, and doting grandmother. She shines a light on what lawyers can do at every stage of their lives, and is bound to inspire you.

While these are the fellow lawyers I admire most, I know there are many others out there deserving of the label "legal hero." And you may be one of them. There is so much at stake in America at this moment. Every one of us must step up.

I hope these stories will inspire you to bring out the hero within you, legal or otherwise.

ONE

My Story - Stepping up in crisis

 Be the change you want to see in the world."

— Mahatma Gandhi

Mahatma Gandhi's famous words reverberated in my mind for days after the November 2016 presidential election.

For over a year, starting in 2015, I had been serving on the Immigration Working Group for Hillary Clinton's presidential campaign. The campaign carefully selected about 30 immigration experts from around the country, and I was privileged to be one. It's one of my proudest accomplishments. We had monthly meetings to discuss immigration issues and prepare for her first 100 days in office. I had so much hope. Hope for the first woman president that would inspire my two daughters. Hope for real immigration reform, finally. Hope for a better world.

The loss felt devastating.

After a week of crying and commiserating with friends, it dawned on me that if I cannot help reform immigration laws at the federal level, I must be ready to help at the local level. States would have to be our shields to whatever policy bullets would come darting from the federal government. Given immigration was Trump's key issue, his policies on immigration actually had potential to impact every aspect of society. Community leaders as well as law and policymakers at all levels of government were going to need immigration law advice. A pathway needed to be created for immigration lawyers to provide guidance.

Within a week, through my local Washington State Chapter of the American Immigration Lawyers Association (AILA WA), I was able to create the Response Committee. My immigration lawyer friends Neha Vyas and Melissa Campos as well as 30 other members joined in to assist.

In the following days, using lessons from the Hillary Clinton campaign, we went to work and started writing memos on topics we thought might be attacked. Simultaneously, I started to spread the word to the local community and especially policy leaders about the Response Committee's offerings of immigration expertise as needed. It was as if my work as a lawyer, radio show host, community volunteer, and immigration advocate had all prepared me for this moment, giving me the foresight and instincts about the steps I needed to take.

And thank goodness we were in position. Five days after Trump's inauguration, on January 25, 2017, he signed two executive orders regarding border security[1] and interior enforcement[2]— paving the way for some of the most inhumane treatment of immigrants seen in modern America. But even more shocking was the travel ban that he signed into effect two days later on the evening of Friday, January 27th.

That was a pivotal moment for lawyers. We took an oath to uphold the rule of law and the Constitution. This moment in history demanded that we each step up as an officer of the court. And step up we did. As protesters descended upon America's airports to decry the travel ban, so did lawyers. No one will soon forget the images of people crowded at airports, shoulder to shoulder. Lawyers sitting on the floor with their laptops, doing legal research and writing motions to file at court.

The shock and outrage were palpable.

There had been no warnings that the order would be signed, or what that would actually mean. It was effective immediately. That meant people already on planes headed to the US were subject to the ban while airborne. People around the world about to embark on their flights to the US were not allowed to board, causing global chaos. And people who had just landed in the US were met with hostility, some hastily being sent back.

Here in Seattle, as soon as the travel ban order was signed, my phone and email exploded. Remember, I had told people that I was ready to help with lawyers if anything happened. I took one last desperate look at my husband's face, and I don't recall seeing him and my children for the next four days. I sat at my dining table fielding phone calls and emails from various organizations, including the Washington Chapter of the Council on American-Islamic Relations, about distressed passengers who'd been impacted by the ban. I fielded requests for legal analysis on immigration law from policymakers.

Most of that week is a blur. I didn't go to the airport. I was behind the scenes doing something more important for my emerging role. Organizing. I recall trying to find a way to create an efficient intake process for the dozens of requests rolling in. Before long I became a Google Forms ninja!

Soon thereafter, my friend, fellow Response Committee member, and immigration lawyer Greg McLawsen introduced me to Takao Yamada, who was leading the volunteer efforts at the Sea-Tac Airport. Greg also informed me that two technology companies, Neota Logic and Clio, had reached out wanting to help. With Greg leading us, Takao, myself, Ryan McClead representing Neota Logic, and Joshua Lenon from Clio, became a team. After I handed over my attempt at creating intake sheets, the team worked around the clock. By the following weekend, airportlawyer.org was live, connecting arriving passengers with legal representation in real time. You can learn more about it from Takao's perspective later in the book.

In the midst of the chaos, I reached out to our AILA WA chapter lawyers to help. Over 50 immigration lawyers stepped up to be part of a roster created and maintained by the law firm Lane Powell to ensure that Sea-Tac Airport was armed with legal experts.

But another problem had surfaced. People in the community were scared — not just undocumented immigrants, but legal immigrants too, as well as people of color, Muslims, and more.

I was getting frequent requests for lawyers to present at "know your rights" events and legal clinics. I became the pestering voice on our Washington chapter AILA listserv, asking people to attend various legal clinics and presentations. To their credit, my fellow immigration lawyers stepped up every single time. The requests would vary — one lawyer here, three lawyers there. The requests were frequent, and continued unabated for almost 18 months.

As the one leading, organizing, and mobilizing our immigration lawyers, I witnessed the incredible generosity of my colleagues, who stepped up over and over to meet the demands of an unprecedented crisis. They wore their hearts on their sleeves and donated their precious time. It is important to note that during this time, all immigration lawyers were contending with the stresses that the administration's adverse policies were already placing on their existing clients and practices. Yet, they still volunteered. For this reason, I feel it is my honor to name and thank every lawyer who helped. You'll find their names in a tribute to my immigration lawyer friends and colleagues in the Special Thanks section at the end of the book.

With so much being demanded of them, naturally, the energy of immigration lawyers to give more to pro bono work was starting to decrease. Yet, all around me, I could see the outrage of other lawyers who didn't specialize in immigration growing, and feeding their desire to help immigrants. I started to ponder on how to bring together these energies.

Given the changing immigration policies that were now

leading to case denials and possible deportation, it was clear that Trump was on a mission to make all his campaign promises come true as fast as possible. You may recall that mass deportation was one such promise. My concern was that if I were suddenly requested by advocacy groups to provide multiple lawyers for immigration court, I would not be able to meet the demand.

Removal or deportation defense work is complicated, challenging, and time-consuming. Cases at court with detained immigrants, especially trials, go beyond the one or two hours that a typical lawyer can commit to pro bono. They require expertise and months of preparation. I knew that there would likely be a time when such a need would arise, and I had to be ready with a solution.

In April 2017, Michael Ramos, the Executive Director of the Church Council of Greater Seattle, asked me to come up with an arrangement for his congregation in case there were increased detentions. That conversation inspired me to research my strategies even further. I started to doodle charts and diagrams for a potential program that would combine the skills of both immigration and non-immigration lawyers to serve immigrants. As my vision got stronger, I got more excited about it.

I didn't intend to start a whole new organization. I intended for someone else to believe in the model and implement it. In hindsight, I learned that if you think you have a brilliant idea, you must be the one to take it to the finish line.

By June 2017, we heard rumors that Trump might rescind the Deferred Action for Childhood Arrival program (DACA). Those rumors gave further urgency to solidify my idea. By September 2017, Trump had done just that, through his then Attorney General Jeff Sessions.

At this point, the idea, which eventually became the Washington Immigrant Defense Network (WIDEN), was still within my committee. But it was time to take it further. What I really wanted was a vehicle to raise funds to distribute to my colleagues who were stepping up repeatedly to do pro bono work without any compensation. If immigration lawyers were asked to fill the gaps time and time again, a blanket demand of their time and expertise was neither feasible nor fair.

After a lot of written proposals, meetings with local leaders, intense debates, and brainstorming with immigration lawyers — and with the invaluable help of my immigration lawyer friend Jay Gairson — the idea took shape. The uncertain element was where and how to house the idea. With a full-time law practice, and two little girls to care for, I didn't want to manage a second organization, especially without knowledge of the nonprofit world.

Around April 2018, we started to hear about children being separated from their parents at the border. I started to have vivid nightmares about children being abused in cells — or even that my own children had been taken away from me. I felt sick to my stomach. I couldn't begin to imagine what the families were going through. I felt the urgency to be ready in case I needed to organize lawyers for immigration court in my local area. I realized by then that I may not have a choice but to create an organization myself.

Sure enough, by June 2018, Washington state received over 200 detained immigrants from the southern border, many of them were parents separated from their children. Detainees were taken to the SeaTac Federal Detention Center because the Northwest Detention Center (NWDC) that houses immigrants was at full capacity. When the news was first released, Washington's 7th Congressional District Representative and long-time immigration advocate Pramila Jayapal went to the Center, a jagged gray structure just under the flight path of planes approaching SeaTac. She had to push her way in, but finally was able to speak to many of the detainees, including mothers separated from their children. They shared horrific stories. I knew then that it was a matter of time before I needed to provide immigration attorneys in large numbers.

On June 9th, 2018, a huge protest was called at the federal detention center by local elected and community leaders. At the protest I ran into Erin Albanese, a corporate and nonprofit law expert whom I'd met a few months prior at a happy hour organized by the secret lawyer mothers group LM. At the protest, I expressed my distress of not having a non-profit platform that I wanted for this very moment.

Once she heard the idea, she asked me, "Well, why haven't you done it yet?"

I told her that I didn't know how to run a non-profit, how to set it up, and just couldn't do it on my own, especially with my full-time job. Later that evening, we met at a kids' playhouse where I brought my files with notes, doodles, and all the research I had accumulated. I explained that while the energy of immigration lawyers was depleted, the outrage of non-immigration lawyers was increasing, with a strong desire to help. Yet without substantive training in immigration law, these lawyers were not able to provide meaningful help. She understood immediately — because she was one of them. And since both she and I were part of the secret group LM, we had both seen the impassioned and horrified reaction of other lawyer mothers, who felt heartbroken and helpless.

After sitting with me for a few hours, she said, "Let me take the nonprofit issues off your hands so you can go do what you need to do."

I felt like crying at that moment. For the first time, someone really understood why this was necessary, why it was urgent, and why this couldn't be an offshoot of another existing nonprofit. It was the first time someone other than Jay really believed in me and the concept. That night, she prepared our nonprofit filing paperwork, taking what she needed from the stack of papers I had accumulated.

The following day, Jay and I met with my friend and co-founder of Airport Lawyer Takao Yamada to discuss the vision and plan. Takao's non-immigration lawyer perspective and his entrepreneurial startup skills were exactly what we needed. Within a week, he was able to get us a logo and website with sign-up sheets for interested lawyers.

In the meantime, my friend and immigration lawyer Minda Thorward, who had been a champion from the start of the idea, agreed to serve on our board. And thus, we became the founding members of this brand-new organization called Washington Immigrant Defense Network — WIDEN. Immigration lawyers and removal defense experts Neha Vyas, Melissa Campos, and Michele Carney agreed to be our advisors. And with my law firm team behind me helping me with operations, we were off and running.

Since the April news of the child separations, there had been outrage and despair in my community. But nowhere was it stronger than within LM — the online lawyer mothers group. The humanitarian crisis was stirring visceral emotions that were unbearable. Like me, many of these women just felt they needed to do something.

On June 21st, 2018, I reached out to the LM network. I was so grateful that many stepped up despite the uncertainty of a brand-new model. Our first cohort from the LM group was Shelly Garzon, Jill Brunner Scott, Cassie Trueblood, Catherine Vyong, and Ashley Fluhrer Greenberg. Others from beyond the group were Joan Tierney, Kelly Vomacka, and Shashi Vijay. The first cohort of immigration lawyers who joined to advise them were my dear friends Melissa Campos, Lourdes Fuentes, Luz Metz, Adam Boyd, and Peggy Herman.

One of the criticisms I'd heard from immigration lawyers when brainstorming the idea was that they could do the work faster themselves, rather than spend time training novices. I needed to overcome the issue. I called upon my AILA WA friend and asylum law expert Kelsey Beckner, who worked with Takao to create a virtual training program. She ensured that our first cohort could be trained as fast as possible.

In the meantime, the Northwest Immigrant Rights Project

(NWIRP) was leading the efforts on the ground to respond to the legal needs of those detainees. Sure enough, that request for multiple courtroom immigration lawyers that I had been expecting finally came. AILA WA lawyers stepped up once again — about 50 members responded to my call to action!

At this point, NWIRP understood the model for WIDEN and began referring cases to our newly formed organization. Finally, the planning of the last 18 months for creating a new model was becoming a reality.

Our first seed funding came from the Washington Chapter of AILA. We were given $10,000 to start the program as a result of advocacy by Jay and myself. The funds allowed us to ensure that our program started off with stipends available for our immigration attorneys, who zealously represented the clients and mentored the non-immigration lawyers.

In January 2019, we held our first large-scale in-person training to a sold-out audience.

It was at this event that Todd Schulte, President of FWD.us, a leading national organization advocating for immigration and criminal justice reform, announced a $25,000 grant for WIDEN. For the last decade, I have advocated for high-skilled immigration reform alongside Todd. As a result, he knew my work and credibility. I was grateful for his trust in me and belief in the program. In recognition of its incredible work and unwavering support of WIDEN, a portion of the proceeds from this book is being donated to the FWD.us Education Fund.

That grant enabled us to continue to take cases. Between August 2018 and February 2020, we trained about 150 non-immigration lawyers in comprehensive immigration removal law. WIDEN drew on that network to provide representation to 15 detained immigrants, just as COVID-19 brought things to a screeching halt, delaying hearings and limiting access to courtrooms.

In the meantime, immigration policy changes continued, causing anxiety to my clients and across the community. The

Executive Director of the Indian Association of Washington (IAWW), Lalita Uppala, reached out requesting immigration lawyers to serve at legal clinics to provide community members free advice on many topics, especially immigration, which had become increasingly fraught under Trump.

The request for immigration lawyers to staff the clinic wasn't remarkable. What was, was the fact that IAWW had funds to pay them. I had been waiting for a moment like this. While trying to raise funds for WIDEN, I attended various roundtables where legal clinic organizers often complained about a dearth of volunteer immigration lawyers. Our time was always strapped, but had become especially so as Trump's policies created wide-scale fear among the immigrant communities.

I realized some form of compensation was necessary if we were going to ensure community members had access to free immigration advice that was so desperately needed. This had all been at the back of my mind, but Lalita paved the way for me to try a new model.

I did what I had become good at — reaching out to my colleagues and asking for help — which they did once again. Lalita and I created an 18-month program for the legal clinic to ensure immigration lawyers were available to the community, and each lawyer was provided a stipend. I filed this success away in my head, hoping that I could duplicate it one clinic at a time when the opportunity arose.

That opportunity was about to arise. In 2017 the Seattle City Council, under the leadership of Council member Lorena Gonzalez, had created a legal defense fund for immigration, and when it was clear DACA was in peril, she was able to advocate for additional funds specifically to assist those clients. Trump had already rescinded the program and the legal battle was pending at the US Supreme Court. It was widely believed that the Supreme Court would side with Trump. Preparation was needed to handle the potential aftermath of such a blow.

The efforts began in October 2019. The City of Seattle Office of Refugee and Immigrant Affairs (OIRA) led by Cuc Vu, brought together local non-profits and stakeholders. Under her brilliant leadership, the City had organized several large-scale legal clinics in the past. The hope was to hold similar events for DACA recipients. With the lessons of the IAWW "low bono" legal clinic example under my belt, and creativity of the Cuc and her team, we agreed that immigration lawyers would receive a stipend for these clinics as well.

Procedurally, we needed someone to administer the funds and house the clinics. I've been a board member with the King County Bar Association (KCBA) for the last couple of years and in that capacity, I was able to reach out to ask for their help. KCBA's Acting Executive Director Anne Daly agreed without hesitation. KCBA, the largest bar association in Washington state, was founded in 1886 to help immigrants being deported as a result of the Chinese Exclusion Act. So it seemed fitting for KCBA to step in, in an equally ugly moment of xenophobia.

OIRA, KCBA, and AILA WA became a dynamic trio, building an innovative approach to broadening access to justice. OIRA was to sponsor the clinics, KCBA to house them, and AILA WA to provide the attorneys. We had 80 lawyers sign up to participate!

While we had held out some hope for it, we couldn't believe the Supreme Court decided in favor of DACA. On June 18th, 2020, they decided that the Trump administration didn't follow the proper rulemaking procedures for terminating the program.

This victory was huge. Immigrant organizers, advocates, and lawyers around the country rejoiced. As a Washingtonian, I am proud of our State Attorney General Bob Ferguson and his team, who played a crucial part in the coalition of states that sued. And our very own AILA WA member Luis Cortes Romero was one of the lead attorneys on the case.

At the time of writing this book, the DACA legal clinic preparations are ongoing, with the anticipation that the administration will likely take further attempts to rescind the program. They've already defied the Supreme Court order to continue accepting new DACA applications.

The formidable team that organized an entirely new and innovative one-of-a-kind clinic were the following: from OIRA- Cuc Vu, Director; Oksana Bilobran, Legal Defense Policy and Program Specialist; Aaliyah Gupta, Consultant; and Meghan Kelly-Stallings, Citizenship Program and Policy Specialist. Anne Daly, Acting Executive Director, and Sarah Villegas, Program Manager of the Neighborhood Legal Clinics, led the efforts of KCBA, with the assistance of volunteer attorney Alex Askerov and volunteer Divya Seth. And of course, Michele Carney and I represented AILA WA.

As 2020 continues, we all find ourselves in a surreal moment in history. We are living in a vortex of complexities. And we have one of the most consequential elections in American history before us. Never before has there been so many reasons to despair, or so much work left to do.

Personally, I've learned a lot of lessons over the last three-and-a-half years that are helping me get through 2020. I've learned that thinking too much can slow me down, and sometimes it's better just to act. I have learned that being a mother is a superpower that gives me the energy to try to make a better world for my daughters. That maternal instincts are a force of nature that can be harnessed to make the world better.

But the biggest lesson is that unprecedented problems require unprecedented solutions. We must be open to new paths. We must be creative and collaborative.

I believe that in the end, we'll find that Hillary Clinton's campaign slogan was indeed true — we truly are *stronger together*.

TWO

Michele Storms - Never resting in the fight for everyone's constitutional rights

W hen talking about fighting for civil rights today, Michele Storms recalls a quote by Charles Hamilton Houston.

Houston, a Black lawyer and professor at Howard University who challenged Jim Crow laws, once said, "A lawyer is either a social engineer… or he's a parasite on society."

Storms is an adherent of the former.

A lawyer, she says, is one who, through the law – whether changing or enforcing it – creates the kind of society we want for everyone.

She has spent 30 years in civil legal aid, as a lawyer, a law professor, and now as the executive director of the ACLU of Washington.

But growing up in San Francisco, being a lawyer was perhaps the farthest thing from her mind. For one thing, she didn't know any. What she knew was what she saw on television – either criminal prosecutors, or big law firms. Neither interested her.

Community service, however, was dear to her heart. She grew up in a family committed to the service of others – and one that occasionally found itself in need of community service itself. So such work became a way of giving back in gratitude for what her family had received as it emerged from poverty.

Storms went to college at Loyola Marymount University in Los Angeles to be in the film and television industry, but she kept a foot still firmly planted in her community.

That brought to her to a transformational event in her life.

She had chosen to live and work in a family homeless shelter, interacting and cooking dinner with the families and children who were residents there. The more she talked to them, the more she realized how sharp and cruel injustice could be. None of these people she encountered had done anything wrong, yet so much wrong had been done to them.

"And as a result, they had no place to be," she says.

That's when she began to get passionate about how she could help struggling communities, and she learned about civil legal aid.

She decided then and there that if the only way she could work on these issues and try to address these problems was to become a lawyer, then that's what she was going to do.

She attended law school at Gonzaga University in Spokane, as a Thomas More Scholar, and after applying for jobs all over the country, landed at Evergreen Legal Services, a civil legal aid organization based in Seattle.

There, she represented domestic violence survivors and worked in domestic and family law.

While Seattle was lucky to have her, Storms also felt lucky to end up in Seattle.

A statewide organization, Evergreen exposed her to the legal community in Washington state, which she soon learned is active in the area of access to justice. She found this community not only passionate, but well-organized and strategic.

"To grow up as a baby lawyer in that context was really incredibly shaping of how my whole career has unfolded," she says.

Efforts at Evergreen to build capacity led to collaborations with private-sector lawyers, law schools, legal clinics, and others interested in fighting for civil rights through the legal system.

Storms soon joined the faculty of the University of Washington Law School, which was expanding its clinical program in family law and domestic violence.

There, she started what was then known as the Child Advocacy Clinic, which represented teenagers in foster care, guardians ad litem, and others in child welfare cases. She loved helping law students see how they could be doing pubic service regardless of what their ultimate career choice might be.

After eight years teaching law, she followed her heart back to legal aid. She worked all over Washington state with groups like Columbia Legal Services and Northwest Justice Project on issues of youth, education, housing, Native American rights, and poverty law.

She returned to the University of Washington Law School as the founding executive director of the Gates Public Service Law program, which was completely focused on public interest law.

For Storms, the new program answered her desire for lawyers to form connections to and perform meaningful service for the people who are the least represented in the legal system.

"I've always felt that law is kind of this closed field, right? To practice law, you have to be a lawyer. And yet, we also know that so many people have legal needs and don't get assistance," she says.

"I was like, let me run that program and get all the law students completely trained up and ready to go and energized and thoughtful about how to make a difference as lawyers in their career."

She headed the Gates Public Service Law program for 10 years and saw numerous students through the program, before being enticed out of the university by an opening for deputy director of the ACLU of Washington.

She started in that position in September 2016, about the time of the presidential debates between Democratic nominee Hillary Clinton and Republican nominee Donald Trump.

As she started, the ACLU national office did something that

Storms says was very smart. They compiled a dossier on both the candidates, on the possible civil rights and civil liberties challenges raised by either potential incoming administration.

Even before the November election, she thought being at the ACLU was exactly the right place to be. Unlike many people in her circle, Storms was not confident of a Clinton victory.

She heard the results at Congresswoman Pramila Jayapal's election night party. While they were excited at Jayapal's victory, the national results were a blow.

"Hearing the news and feeling just a little bit of a knot in the stomach, like what's ahead for us?" she recalls.

The ACLU is a nonpartisan organization, committed to holding government accountable to the rule of law, and has held all administrations accountable. Storms was troubled by Trump's campaign promises, especially on immigration.

After the election, ACLU-WA sprang into action, hiring an immigration law specialist and coordinating with the national office on the expected assaults on immigration and on reproductive rights.

"I remember we had a lot of conversations at the local and national level about the Supreme Court and what to expect there," she says.

The ACLU had a number of cases lined up with the expectation – which proved accurate – that the Supreme Court and the federal court system would be reconfigured with more conservative justices.

Fortunately, civil rights and civil liberties cases can also be heard by state courts.

"In Washington state, we just have a wonderful judiciary, we have such a strong and thoughtful state Supreme Court," she says. "We knew that the federal judiciary was going to change and might not change in a very good direction for civil rights and civil liberties."

All of this planning was just in preparation for Trump's inauguration.

"We didn't know what would really actually happen," she says. "But in January, we found out."

With Trump's sudden ban on travelers from majority Muslim countries, lawyers scrambled to Sea-Tac International Airport, and across the country, to defend the rights of people who had been blocked from legal entry into the country.

"That's a weekend that I will never in all my life forget," she says.

One of the ACLU's cases involved a refugee from Somalia.

His family had been in refugee camps in Kenya and had spent months going through the legal and logistical processes, preparing to join him in the United States. Their reunion was blocked by Trump's ban.

"This was something that was impacting many, many families, where all the paperwork and all the medical visits and all the things that you have to do, there's so much," she says.

The ACLU won that case, and has helped many other refugee families to reunite.

But those victories are cold comfort in the face of ongoing oppression of immigrants and refugees.

Storms says she's troubled by the Immigration and Customs Enforcement and the Customs and Border Protection officers' practice of boarding domestic Greyhound buses and demanding to see passengers' identification.

"Nobody's going to Canada or Mexico or anything. It was basically, like Yakima to Missoula, Montana, or something like that. And they were getting on the buses and asking people to show their papers, which is so disturbing," she says.

"It's reminiscent of apartheid South Africa, where people were required to carry papers. And of course," she adds, "they were specifically asking people with brown skin who weren't speaking English."

Storms believes another big threat to immigrant civil rights is the Trump administration's attempt to integrate immigration enforcement with local law enforcement.

The ACLU of Washington state has tried to get local police agencies not to collaborate with federal immigration agencies. The organization lobbied for the Keep Washington Working Act, which, among other things, restricts the extent to which local law enforcement agencies cooperate in the enforcement of federal immigration laws.

The act, which also has been couched as a commerce-related act that encourages the development of programs and policies to help immigrants working in and supporting Washington industries, passed in 2019.

"It's helpful that people can just live their lives and go to work and pay their taxes and do all the things that immigrants do and citizens do, without that harassment," Storms says.

The ACLU-WA has been busy on all fronts for the past three years – including appointing Storms as executive director in 2019.

In that time, other perennial ACLU issues have been threatened by the Trump administration, including reproductive rights; access to maternal and family care; and care for lesbian, gay, and transgender people.

And though Storms praises Washington state for having many strong jurists and policies, there are still state issues that concern her. One is the state's three strikes law, which imposes life in prison without the possibility of parole for people with three felony convictions. Another is the state's incarceration of youth, and especially long sentences.

George Floyd's murder and the Black Lives Matter protests in the summer of 2020 were a catalyst for further action. The ACLU filed a lawsuit against the city of Seattle for the police department's use of tear gas and other crowd control weapons during the protests.

"One of America's original pandemics is racism. And the way that shows up in policing is becoming ever more evident to people, particularly after what happened to George Floyd, which was nothing short of torture," she says. "It's our right to say that government is being too heavy-handed – literally has its knee on our neck. Standing up for that is what the ACLU was absolutely founded for."

Storms says that a growing number of Americans are having their eyes opened to the systemic racism in law enforcement and the nation's institutions.

"People are more and more cognizant that, no, this isn't just a random thing, this is a deeply embedded problem," she says. "People are speaking out."

Storms says that she finds the practice of law much different from the stereotype of a staid and formal practice. She sees it as a vital tool in the grassroots fight for justice.

"In these days, in particular, with COVID-19, with racism, with all the things that we've been talking about, lawyers can bring this special tool of the law to try to make change for the better, for everyone, so that we can all live free," she says.

"I would say people have gotten pretty laser-focused on making sure that we can preserve democracy and preserve our rights," she says, reflecting on the last three-and-a-half years under Trump.

The ACLU has certainly had more volunteer attorneys than in years past.

"We've had a lot of people come to us and say we will help in whatever way," she says. "People are interested in using the skills and tools that we have as lawyers to fight for freedom and for rights."

Storms advises lawyers who want to get involved to find organizations such as the Northwest Immigrant Rights Project, Columbia Legal Services, and Northwest Justice Project, to learn more about their areas of specialty.

"And if you want to work in an area that you haven't worked in before, think about some CLEs [continuing legal education classes], and help us to be able to use you better," she says.

She says that many lawyers can also educate themselves on

anti-racism, and the history of racism and the nativist, anti-immigrant sentiment that still pervades this country.

"When people want to do immigration work or do the criminal legal work, I think it's helpful to work with protesters to understand the context in which people find themselves in need," she says.

She sees today's legal fights as stemming from the very founding of this country – created with an ideal of civil rights that was not always met.

"All of our rights, all the things that the Constitution promised us, when it was written it was only meant to apply to a select few. We embrace that it must apply to every single one of us, regardless of our color or gender or whoever we are," Storms says.

"That freedom is the essence of what we need to be as Americans living on this soil. And that is what we are fighting for."

THREE

Matt Adams - The unifying fight to protect immigrant rights

W henever there's a battle against government overreach, you can reliably find Matt Adams on the frontlines. As legal director for the Northwest Immigrant Rights Project, he says that's where the fight against authoritarianism happens. It's the only place to be when a presidential administration is declaring war on democracy itself.

"They really are doing what they can to take us away from a democracy," he says bluntly.

You can tell Adams isn't just tossing around matches and trying to start a fire. This man is genuinely worried about the next fight, and he's already reaching for a weapon.

But his battle against injustice didn't begin with Donald Trump. During the Obama years, NWIRP under Adams' leadership was fighting for humanitarian issues like the right to legal representation for immigrants with mental or psychological disabilities. In that particular case, Adams helped represent almost 200 disabled immigrants in Arizona, California, and Washington who did not have the right to appointed counsel. Eventually, US District Judge Dolly Gee, of the Central District of California rendered a decision in favor of his clients, and the Obama administration chose not to appeal it.

The victory earned Adams the Washington State Bar Association's Award of Merit in 2016.

And then, a few weeks later, Trump happened.

Adams says he was in the middle of a soccer game when he learned the election was going south. His wife had suggested planning a small party at the house with friends, but Adams was too nervous about what election night might bring. The political wind was suddenly turning sour.

His nose had picked up something ugly weeks earlier.

Adams, born in Hood River, Oregon, grew up in White Salmon and Ridgefield, Washington. After graduating from law school he moved to Yakima, Washington. During those early years, he'd developed a feel for rural sentiment, to the point where he already feared where the country was headed, well before election night. He knew the rhetoric that had fueled Trump's campaign well. He recognized the venom and the tactics.

Consequently, he also knew to expect an increase in his legal workload after the election.

"The week that Trump was inaugurated, we filed our first lawsuit, which was *Wagafe v. Trump.*"

Wagafe is a class action suit challenging a secret federal program called Controlled Application Review and Resolution Program (CARRP), which blocks certain immigrant applications through malevolent stalling. The program exists *specifically* to deny or indefinitely delay the applications of thousands of law-abiding immigrants through the use of intentionally vague and shifty parameters. Its byzantine mechanics target a very specific kind of victim.

United States Citizenship and Immigration Service (USCIS) began the policy in 2008, so its illegality actually precedes the day-to-day illegitimacy of the Trump administration. The program is an agency-wide policy to "identify, process, and adjudicate certain immigration applications that allegedly raise national security concerns."[1] To some that probably sounds like a perfectly legitimate extra step for vetting people entering the country in a post-September 11 world. But that deliberately ambiguous use of the phrase "national security concern" is where things get ugly.

"National security" can be predicated upon whether or not an applicant is on a government "terrorist watchlist." Adams says different government agencies compile several different lists with some overlap, but none of them match and most paint with very broad strokes. Conservative writer Stephen F. Hayes, for example, was on one such terror watchlist in 2016.[2] Reporter Dave Lindorff—who wrote about the United States' inhumane use of torture during the Iraq War—was on another in 2019.[3] The list concerning CARRP contains up to a million people, and it includes folks allegedly "associated" with anyone already on the list, even if the original watch-lister had never legitimately earned a place on it.[4]

Adams says the CARRP program primarily targets Muslims. It doesn't matter if its victims are going through the asylum process because their home government is in chaos or they have a target on their back. It doesn't matter if applicants already have their green cards and are seeking naturalization.

Any program making use of such a subjective list already has a shaky foundation, but organizations like the ACLU and Northwest Immigrant Rights Project say CARRP was adopted without any congressional approval or public comment. Both organizations claim it vehemently violates the Fifth Amendment's guarantee of due process, since nobody is told why their application has been stalled. Nor are they given a proper opportunity to clear their names. There's no CARRP court. You are "convicted" with the covert finality of a grudging bride and groom wiping you off a wedding invite list.

Although started in 2008, Adams says CARRP did not become generally known until after litigation challenging the government's failure to respond to Freedom of Information Act (FOIA) requests ripped it from the shadows. Since then, immigrants' rights advocates have filed many individual challenges to CARRP, but they've all been "mooted out," he says, before the courts could address the merits of the program. The election of Trump, and his numerous threats to ban Muslims, made it clear to NWIRP lawyers that they needed a strong class action approach to head off any federal efforts to expand the program.

Adams's organization and the ACLU, along with other partners, have now been litigating the case for four years, using the court in *Wagafe v. Trump* to bring daylight to this secret net blocking thousands from immigration benefits that they are otherwise entitled to.

Wagafe is just one fight among many, however. Adams and his allies have been challenging the administration's grotesque actions nonstop for nearly three years, from illegally harassing immigrants without cause, to flagrantly endangering noncitizen detainees amid the COVID-19 pandemic. [5]

Trump's crusade to cut immigrant children from their parents is one battle that makes Adams particularly frustrated.

In early 2018, the administration bragged about a new zero-tolerance policy toward immigrant families attempting to illegally cross the US border. The tactic involved targeting families that were detained while crossing the border to seek asylum and other forms of protection. Customs and Border Protection (CBP) officers physically separated children from their parents and then held the adults in CBP facilities, detention centers, and federal prisons, while their children were taken away and dumped in makeshift tent cities[6] or sent to juvenile facilities across the country.

A large proportion of the people being impacted were never actually *criminally* prosecuted. Those that were usually managed to wrap their cases up within three or four days, primarily because prosecutors could only hit them for criminal entry, a misdemeanor.

Adams says he and other lawyers recognized the policy of separating parents from their children as a punitive measure to deter people, many of whom were fleeing persecution in their own country.

They had to watch with horror as hundreds of children got shipped to places as far away as New York while their parents stewed in places like the SeaTac federal prison, near Seattle, waiting for a hearing without the benefit of a lawyer.[7]

Once images of kids in cages hit the news, a federal district court in California issued an injunction demanding the government begin the process of reuniting broken families.[8]

Adams and his crew were already looking beyond the separation policy, however. Amid the chaos of immigrant kidnapping, an additional pressing issue was slipping past the news reports.

People apprehended near the border aren't guaranteed due process of a trial. Most never even see an immigration judge. Instead, they get an expedited removal order from border patrol.

The only thing that can interrupt this quick removal is an asylum claim — an immigrant's credible fear of what may happen to them if they go back to their home country. Whether or not Trump likes it, the US government must abide by its own laws and international treaties guaranteeing them the right to apply for asylum.

In that case, the law states an asylum officer should screen the applicant and determine whether or not there is credible fear. If the applicant makes a convincing case, he or she goes before an immigration judge and gets a full and fair hearing before a court.

But Trump's crew threw a brick into that process by locking people up for weeks or months before they got the asylum interview. On top of that, many of the refugees were forcibly separated from their children without knowledge of their whereabouts. Those circumstances were enough to force countless legitimate asylum seekers to surrender their rights and return to the vicious cartels, gang violence, and oppressive governments that awaited them.

Adams and NWIRP launched a suit, *Padilla v. ICE*, challenging the delays in the asylum interviews, and demanding the administration provide prompt bond hearings to asylum seekers. They eventually won a decision in US District Court in Seattle on behalf of a nationwide class, challenging the administration's violations of the due process clause, the Immigration and Nationality Act, and the Administrative Procedure Act.

Attorney General William Barr responded with a move to deny bond hearings entirely, arguing immigration judges don't have the authority to conduct bond hearings in which respondents can seek release from detention.[9] The Ninth Circuit Court of Appeals issued a preliminary injunction rejecting Barr's argument in July 2019, and it upheld its decision in March 2020.[10][11][12] But in late August the Acting Solicitor General filed a petition for certiorari, asking the United States Supreme Court to review the decision, making it clear that the fight is far from over. In the meantime, thousands of asylum seekers continue to receive bond hearings. Call it a tentative success.

Even when big decisions go in favor of immigrants, the "win" can be tenuous. As of July 2020, the administration continued to flout one Supreme Court order compelling the full restoration of the Deferred Action for Childhood Arrivals (DACA), which the administration tried to rescind in its first year in office. Former President Barack Obama had launched the program in 2012 as a kind of half-solution to the issue of immigrants who came to the United States at a young age, and who now view the US as more of a home than the nation their parents fled. While not providing a direct path to citizenship, it entitles them to social security numbers so they can work and study without fear of running afoul of US Immigration and Customs Enforcement and being deported.

The Migration Policy Institute believes that there are nearly 650,000 people who already benefit from DACA and that there are probably more than 1.3 million potential beneficiaries still out there — unconfirmed.

Trump ran on a campaign of deporting DACA youth, however, and his Department of Homeland Security moved to end the program by June of his first year. The Northwest Immigrant Rights Project, with many other partners, challenged the move. By September, almost 20 states, along with the District of Columbia, had filed a suit, *New York v. Trump*, in US District Court in New York to halt the repeal.

Not surprisingly, California also put its power behind the attack, since one-quarter of DACA beneficiaries live in that state. The University of California, with its roughly 4,000 undocumented students, refused to be left out of the fight and filed its own suit against the Department of Homeland Security in US District Court. Every court decision challenged the president over the means by which he had moved to scrub the program. Eventually the battle arrived on the doorstep of the Supreme Court, which in June 2020 ruled the administration's actions against the DACA program "arbitrary and capricious" in *Department of Homeland Security v. Regents of the University of California.*

The SCOTUS decision on DACA was a welcome, if stunning, surprise. Still, it was clear at the time of this writing that the Trump administration was openly defying it, saying they would simply stop accepting new DACA applications.

Despite the administration's infuriating lack of respect for the law, Adams says the real high point of the DACA fight was the amount of unity that it cultivated. The majority of the success of the program had less to do with the finesse of lawyers and more to do with widespread support from the community. Its saving grace, he claims, was the sheer organization and activism of the followers crowding in behind it.

This, he adds, can be said of much of what Trump does.

"You know, I think one of the silver linings behind this horrific era that we've gone through under the Trump administration is the coming together of the different communities working to fight for civil rights and justice," Adams says.

People, he explains, are generally stuck in their individual silos of activism. Some may be focused upon immigrants' rights, others on environmental justice, and still others on LGBTQ rights. There is occasional overlap, but most enclaves are thoroughly absorbed in their own fights.

The broader community may not have thought so much about immigration before the Trump administration made it a No. 1 target. But Trump's apparent war on nearly everybody, and democracy itself, appears to have aligned a formerly fragmented community in a battle that wasn't so universally embraced a few years ago.

In that sense, Trump proved to be the ultimate unifier.

FOUR

Traci Feit Love - A visionary vehicle for legal volunteerism

Traci Feit Love says she regrets the years when she "had the privilege of disconnecting from politics."

But like for many others, the election results of 2016 were a wake-up call. Love was immediately compelled to take action.

Her story is exceptional for how immediately, and how deeply, she plunged into activism. Her efforts over the past 3-and-a-half years have brought together tens of thousands of lawyers and supporters to defend human rights, resist governmental abuses of power, and strengthen democratic institutions.

Love always had an interest in the fight for justice and equality under the law. As a women's studies major at the University of Delaware, she worked with survivors of sexual assault, and founded the university's first gender equity group (which remains active more than 20 years later). As a law student at Harvard, she researched the impact of the War on Drugs on women, and was struck by the obvious racial disparities, hoping she would have an opportunity to tackle such issues in her legal career.

But after a few years as a commercial litigation associate at DLA Piper's Boston office — and especially after the birth of her daughter — her focus shifted primarily to supporting herself and her family while being able to work from home. Over the next decade, she leveraged her experience and technical skills to become something of a communications and social media wizard, providing digital marketing and consulting services to law firms.

That path changed dramatically in 2016.

On the day of the presidential election, Love and her eight-year-old daughter, Carly, spent the day shopping for their own small election night party for two. The idea was to celebrate what they thought would be the election of the first woman president.

"I was naively optimistic about the outcome of the election," says Love, "and I got my daughter really excited about it as well."

The plans for celebration were premature.

As the two of them watched the election results come in, Love's daughter asked her, "What are we going to do now?"

"She'd heard all of my commentary over the course of the campaign about the rhetoric that was coming out of the Trump campaign," says Love. "And so she was genuinely scared, which I think reflected my fear about what a Trump presidency might mean for civil and human rights in our country."

At that time, Love was working for a company providing online reputation management for law firms. Expertise in marketing, digital media, mass communications, and working with remote teams was her jam.

So it was natural for her to sit down at the computer that night.

She went to Facebook groups, composed mostly of women who had been talking on social media over the course of the election. A few hours of sleep, and she was back online, to the virtual spaces where people were commiserating about the results of the election — and sharing very emotional responses.

Then, says Love, "I started noticing a pattern."

For every 10 or 15 posts of people expressing anger and

dismay and devastation, Love says she would see a different kind of post from a lawyer.

"Usually it was a woman lawyer, because that's who was in these groups I was part of," she explains. "Someone would come into the group and say, 'Okay, we need to organize. Here are some things I think we need to do.' And it would be, you know, five-step action plans, 10 ideas, really meaningful ideas all over the spectrum."

Watching these suggestions for practical action show up in the feed but then get buried under more commiseration, Love wondered if she could bring lawyers together to take action. She started with a Facebook post:

> *Friends/Family: If you (1) have a law degree, and (2) aren't happy with how the election turned out, and (3) would like to contribute your knowledge/skills/support towards a better future, please add a comment here and I'll send you an invitation to a like-minded group forming now. If not, feel free to ignore this message.*

"I thought I was going to get 25-30 attorneys into a group," says Love. But people started sharing her posts and inviting others to the group. Within 72 hours, 60,000 lawyers had joined. In three weeks, there were 125,000 — or as Love puts it, "10 percent of the nation's lawyers."

That was the genesis of Lawyers for Good Government (L4GG) and the L4GG Foundation, affiliated non-profit organizations whose shared mission is to protect and strengthen democratic institutions, resist abuse of power and corruption, and defend the rights of those who suffer in the absence of good government.

"It so quickly became something so different from what I

envisioned that it required a complete overhaul of my life," says Love.

She decided to put everything she had into figuring out how to maximize the potential of the dynamic army of lawyers who had answered the call of her Facebook post. It was a risky move, but Love decided to quit her job to organize the group full-time. Fortunate to have her family's backing, plunging into a new area of work was still a frightening dive into the unknown for Love, who by this time was a single mom and sole breadwinner.

"It was terrifying, but it also didn't really feel like a choice," she says. "It just felt like something I had to do. And I believed that with this much energy and this much support, there had to be a way."

How do you organize 125,000 people, let alone lawyers, when time is of the essence and momentum is vital? Love started by asking questions about what it would take to turn a Facebook group into a high-impact organization for legal action. She made it her business to learn from activists, organizers, and people who had experience running nonprofits. There were conversations that went on for hours, often with new contacts, the "incredible people" who stepped up to become her collaborators and colleagues.

A lot of what they did in the beginning was "like a market assessment," says Love: understanding what other organizations were already doing, what the members of the group were looking for, how people wanted to be involved, and where the most urgent unmet needs were. She began with surveys asking just those questions — including a survey completed by more than 15,000 lawyers.

In the lead-up to the inauguration, Love's nascent organization focused on putting together a conference called "Rise Above" for lawyers and activists, to take place in DC right after the Women's March. A thousand people from L4GG showed up to march together, and about 1,100 people attended the "Rise Above" conference the next day.

"That was when a lot of us realized this would become much more than a Facebook group," says Love. "We became a real community."

That community got to work when President Trump's Muslim Ban was announced a week later. Thousands of lawyers were suddenly needed to handle pro bono immigration cases around the country. The L4GG Facebook group became a coordinating hub overnight for lawyers who were showing up at airports and trying to make a difference.

"I didn't know it when we started," says Love, "but one of our greatest strengths as an organization is mobilizing lawyers quickly in response to a crisis situation."

It's a good thing, because responding quickly and effectively was crucial as the new administration presented one crisis after another.

"When I look back," says Love, "the whole thing feels very blurry. Just a whirlwind of activity, so many conversations, very little sleep. But it was also one of the most exciting times of my life because there was so much potential to make a difference."

One of the biggest challenges for Love was figuring out where to focus the group's attention.

When she initially surveyed her members, she asked what areas they most wanted to focus on: Immigration? Human rights? Climate change? Racial justice? Corruption? It turned out the answer was "all of the above"— the lawyers who responded had a hard time prioritizing with so many important issues on the table. So Love and her team learned to look for where there was immediate need and their group had specific skills and assets to contribute.

Immigration was and continues to be one such area of huge need, where pro bono lawyers can make a real difference. In 2018, when news investigations spotlighted both the cruelty of the family separation policy that took children away from parents seeking refuge in the United States, and the abysmal conditions in immigrant detention centers, L4GG started their immigrants' rights program, Project Corazon.[1] Once again, Love and her colleagues were aware of the importance of working with those who were already experts in the field.

In partnership with RAICES, Project Corazon began to provide remote legal representation to asylum seekers during their "credible fear interviews" (a screening process during which asylum seekers must convince officials that they should be allowed to continue with their asylum claim). Since the program began, more than 1,500 asylum seekers detained at the Karnes Detention Center in South Texas have received representation — all remotely — during their credible fear interviews.

Project Corazon has also partnered with the Immigration Justice Campaign, CLINIC, and other legal services organizations to provide assistance with asylum applications, bond and parole cases, BIA appeals, and other forms of legal support for asylum seekers. In addition, through the Project Corazon Travel Fund, L4GG has been able to send hundreds of lawyers and law students to the border and detention centers across the country to offer pro bono services to asylum seekers.

In 2019, with funding from a grassroots campaign, L4GG set up the first full-time US immigration legal clinic for asylum seekers in Mexico. The Matamoros clinic is led by program director Charlene D'Cruz, a bilingual immigration attorney who relocated to Brownsville, Texas, just across the border, to do the work. When COVID-19 hit, they did what L4GG has gotten good at — they responded nimbly to the crisis. They're handling intakes and screening, reviewing files, and handling immigration appeals by mobilizing pro bono attorneys from all over the US — all remotely, and safely, over the internet.

At a time when there is great need for such legal help, L4GG has become a way for many lawyers to do the pro bono work that is a particularly effective form of activism. They've set up legal clinics in 10 states to help small businesses and organizations stay afloat during the pandemic — providing advice on applying for grants and loans, negotiating commercial leases, and handling other legal issues. They also do a lot of work in the area of climate change, under the leadership of environmental lawyer Jillian Blanchard. Through their climate change program, L4GG pro bono attorneys provide legal research and guidance to municipal governments interested in transitioning to 100 percent renewable energy.

Most recently, L4GG launched their Lawyers for Racial Justice (LRJ) program in partnership with law firms and in-house legal departments across the country. Through the LRJ program, pro bono attorneys will research and draft model legislation designed to help bring about systemic change at the state and local level. This focus on systemic change represents an important expansion of L4GG's work into the world of policy and will be led by Adam Fernandez, L4GG's new Vice President of Policy and Strategic Engagement.

"To me," says Love, "activism is when you're taking a stand and taking action to effect change."

That might mean helping one asylum-seeking family in Matamoros, or fighting for policy changes to help thousands or even millions of people.

"Every lawyer doing that work is a hero in my book," says Love.

And she hopes as many as possible keep doing it — activist lawyers are a valuable resource. Though there are about 1.25 million lawyers in the US, some are retired, some in law school, and some are just starting out. So for all of the issues, and all of the legal areas that need some type of help, "there's really a fixed number of us to go around. So it takes all of us doing whatever we can, and bringing whatever we can to the table."

Her goal for L4GG is to inspire and empower as many lawyers as possible to get involved and make a difference, whether through pro bono work, advocacy, or activism more generally.

"Sometimes it's volunteering to take an immigration case, sometimes it's doing pro bono research, sometimes it's advocating for policy changes. And sometimes, quite frankly, it's donating to and supporting the organizations that are doing the work," she says. "I never want any lawyer to think that a donation doesn't count or doesn't make a difference, because everything we do is made possible by those donations."

Love knows that people sometimes hesitate to take action because they feel overwhelmed by how much needs to be done. Her advice is to get into the fray and be persistent when volunteering to help beleaguered organizations. To understand that even organizations that really need your legal skills may take some time figuring out how to utilize them. And to resist the feeling that you have to take on all the problems at once.

"It's perfectly fine to choose one issue area where you feel like you can make a difference, because it's not about what any *one* of us is doing. It's about what *all* of us collectively are doing," she says.

"So here's my most important piece of advice: choose something, and then get started."

FIVE

Margaret O'Donnell - Bringing shadowy immigration courts under the lights of the stage

M argaret O'Donnell has always been a storyteller.
Back home in Appalachia, her family would gather on warm summer evenings beneath a streetlight and tell stories.

That passion put her on a career path to journalism. In the 1970s she worked as a reporter for newspapers in Indiana. Portraying the world in words was useful, and O'Donnell had a knack for it.

But she had an itch to better understand the mechanics of government and politics. A law degree delivered the best skill set for that kind of comprehension. So, in her late 20s, she veered toward law and immigration, where the former reporter found some very jarring stories indeed.

Up until then, O'Donnell had lived in a segregated world with very little exposure to immigrants. The first pro bono case she took as a lawyer was an asylum seeker from El Salvador, at the height of the Reagan era interventions in Central and South America.

From that case on, the direction of her career was cemented.

She was fascinated, she says, by the courage, the ambition, the skill, and sheer energy it took to be an immigrant, to leave one's home and create a new life for oneself in a new country.

She was equally horrified by the brutality of the system, and the Reagan regime's approach toward asylum seekers.

The 1980s were a time of oppression and murder in El Salvador and Guatemala, as military-backed oligarchies pillaged their nation's wealth and violently eliminated all opposition. This was not long after the Carter administration and Congress had passed the Refugee Act, a humanitarian law that finally brought the US into compliance with international human rights standards.

President Ronald Reagan quickly undermined Carter's work and international law, however, by mislabeling Salvadorans and Guatemalans as "economic migrants," just so his administration could deny that the Guatemalan and Salvadoran governments were violating human rights.[1] This denial changed the status of the battered refugees seeking asylum in America, and it allowed the US to reduce approval rates for Salvadoran and Guatemalan asylum cases, all the way to under 3 percent in 1984.[2]

The sheer depth of ruthlessness from her own government became inversely proportional to O'Donnell's own desire to counter it, and it pulled her into the immigration courts for decades. In 2009 she founded Global Law Advocates, an immigration law firm that handles legal residence petitions, immigration court defense, visas, and naturalization matters, among other things.

O'Donnell didn't choose her career for the string of victories it promised. Attorneys often beat their heads against legal walls like the ones barring asylum-seekers for years, without much success. But occasionally they surprise everyone and knock down a wall.

Consider the asylum abuses of the Reagan regime: O'Donnell says attorneys' success rate was low, but they still did the very best job they could, and because of their hard work they eventually gathered and catalogued enough information to help establish the *American Baptist Churches v. Thornburgh* (ABC) Settlement Agreement 10 years later.

Even today, that agreement prevents eligible class members whose asylum claims were denied in the 1980s and early 1990s from being deported until they've had an opportunity to obtain a new asylum interview and a new decision under the Nicaraguan Adjustment and Central American Relief Act (NACARA).[3]

Just like the 1980s, however, the Trump era has proved to be a dispiriting time to be an immigration attorney. O'Donnell says the situation is actually worse now, because many South American and Central American asylum seekers today don't get the benefit of a court date. They don't even have the ability to be in the country in order to present their claim, despite this being an alleged guarantee under our nation's asylum treaties. The system, she says, is politically rigged. Bureaucrats, under the marching orders of the Trump White House, have reduced the letter of a law designed to be just and fair to a farce.

It's easy to get cynical under these conditions, and that's precisely what O'Donnell did following the election of Donald Trump in 2016, as a string of nativist decisions poured from the White House, aiming to reverse years of progress O'Donnell and others had fought for since the 1980s. From Trump's first move to hold noncitizens from majority-Muslim nations hostage in airports, to his push to scrap noncitizens from the 2020 Census, Trump has had a way of exhausting the very souls of humanitarians.[45]

By 2019, O'Donnell's paralegals were sounding the alarm on the dangerous pathos threatening to envelop her just prior to her retirement.

In hopes of lifting her spirits, they reminded her of one of her more inspirational moments.

In a fit of fury following the 2016 election, O'Donnell called her office together and delivered a rousing vow: "Fight every case, twice as hard." Because their clients needed them now more than ever.

"We are not giving up," she'd sworn.

Those words stuck with her coworkers and strengthened them at a moment of great despair.

And yet, two years into Trump's term, O'Donnell herself had lost sight of them.

Her paralegals gave her a much-needed jolt. They reminded her of the necessity of the fight, and that the fight was what it was really all about. People have fists for a *reason*.

O'Donnell reasoned that unprecedented times required a new tactic. The White House was using the loudest voice in the nation to demonize immigrants. To fight back would require ripping off the ugly mask the president was trying to hang on millions of innocent people.

Falling back on her career as a journalist, O'Donnell set out to show Americans what was really going on in the nation's immigration courts.

Between 2007 and 2019, O'Donnell had regularly produced bilingual "Know Your Rights" presentations to circulate around the state of Washington. But she came to realize that her audience just wasn't getting the gist of things from a PowerPoint. There's only so much that can be conveyed with statistics, figures, and a string of legalese and state laws.

O'Donnell wanted to move the plight of non-immigrants to the kind of passion that drives real change. She had considered several different formats to deliver the feelings behind the fact. A game show idea morphed into an improv troupe.

But legal drama couldn't be delivered properly without a script. The specific truths behind the stories were all-important. It was the human experiences that enraged.

Some fellow immigration attorneys — who were also living the misery of watching innocent clients get ripped away from their lives and families — had plenty of their own narratives to contribute.

The Detention Lottery and *Detained* are two of her productions that grew from this workshop-style process.[6] Both are interactive dramas featuring audience volunteers and a Q&A session.

The trick, O'Donnell found, was conveying the despair of the immigration process, without inundating the audience and making them shut down. The attorneys decided to distill a small portion of all that agony and malpractice down to one typical hour in an immigration court. A sort of spin on the 1980s comedy "Night Court," but with more inhumanity and a lot fewer laughs.

The Detention Lottery is designed to put the viewer in the shoes of an immigrant facing the infuriating Catch-22 that Uncle Sam usually reserves for non-citizens.[7] The play, like her other stage-targeted creations, makes clear that this brand of court was never truly created to dispense justice.

"ICE hasn't given me your file," a private attorney informs the actor portraying Jose Miguel, a real character with his name changed for the stage, who is yanked from his car and put before a judge for his first hearing. "I won't get it until we're in court and maybe not even then. New policy."

Miguel learns that his single best tool for defending himself in a courtroom environment — preparation — just got snatched away.

"I see that you have a DUI from seven years ago," the attorney says. "That might be a reason why you were detained. … I know they're getting people with old convictions."

"I completed all the classes, I paid all the fines," Miguel argues. "It's closed… I've been in this country almost 30 years! My wife too… How much is the bond?"

"It'll probably be $15,000."

Poor Miguel runs that number through his head, wondering if the lawyer stuttered and dumped in an extra zero by accident. "What? We don't have that kind of money!" he shouts.

"Almost nobody does," the lawyer admits. "You may have to put your house up as a guarantee. We're going to be lucky to get any bond at all."

"This judge hates DUIs," the lawyer hurriedly tacks on, trying to be helpful. "Be sure to show remorse for the DUI."

Things go downhill for Miguel from there. To an audience of American-born citizens, the immigration legal process looks nothing at all like the justice system that we came to know from all those Perry Mason shows. But that's kind of the point, according to O'Donnell.

"Theater is a heart-opener, a mind-opener in ways that nothing else touches, not film, not academic presentations, not even real-life experience, at times," O'Donnell says. "It distills actuality and makes it realer than real. That's why I write plays about the immigrant experience, so those of us who aren't immigrants can see and feel and taste what it might be like to live in the funhouse distortion of a justice system that immigration courts are."

Nothing is fabricated in the script, except names. Actual attorneys play the characters. In fact, in the troupe of 12 players, everybody but two actors are immigration attorneys. Random spectators get snatched from the audience and put through the wringer. It's a frightening, dehumanizing experience

In addition to *The Detention Lottery* and *Detained*, O'Donnell also wrote another play about the nightmarish immigrant experience of immigration court proceedings: *Undocumented*, which was produced in 2016. She has written several other plays, which have progressed to various stages of production.[8] At the end of each show, there's an interactive talkback session with the audience. Much of that talkback, she says, pertains to how horrified the audience is by the speed with which immigration court bounces people back to their home countries, regardless of the threat that awaits them there, or the disruption in their families, which are often a mix of naturalized US citizens and non-citizens.

O'Donnell says that within 18 months, the outrage of *The Detention Lottery* had moved viewers to donate thousands of dollars for legal services and immigrant groups looking to improve the system, including the Washington Immigration Solidarity Alliance Network and the Northwest Immigrant Rights

Project.[910] After the play's pilot production in June 2018, community groups, schools, and churches stepped in and began producing it themselves. O'Donnell and her troupe averaged one presentation a month in and around the Seattle area before the onset of COVID-19.

While writing plays might not be for everyone, O'Donnell says there are plenty attorneys can do to make a difference. Discover what you are most passionate about, be it immigration, environmental protection, or the Black Lives Matter movement, and volunteer your time to it. She reminds attorneys that they don't even need to be that experienced to have an impact, thanks to the intimidating amount of paralegal work that needs doing. Do you like to write briefs? Well, lucky you, there's an army of briefs awaiting your attention, in any given direction.

It's entirely too much work for O'Donnell to simply walk away from, even after her recent retirement. She says she'll continue to recruit attorneys for pro bono work, but she'll also keep working to help the public comprehend the injustice underway each day in the nation's immigration courts, just outside of view.

"Art is the best way to open hearts and minds," she says. "When we know where injustice hides — when the detention doors are open to us at last — we can look in and know that we must make changes."

SIX

Jill Scott - Of borders, bravery, and bearing witness

G rowing up in Fairbanks, Alaska, Jill Scott never wanted to be a lawyer.

Both of her parents were public-interest lawyers, and she still remembers being lulled to sleep at the dinner table by their discussions of motions, briefings and depositions.

"I remember being a kid, bored and annoyed, as my sister and I worked in our coloring books and played go-fish in the dingy waiting room at the jail while my public defender mom met with clients," Scott says.

But as Scott studied microbiology as an undergraduate, the advantages of legal insight became more apparent to her. She was passionate about global health policy and she often wondered what it would be like to be in the room when policy decisions about science and healthcare were made.

She couldn't have known then that her unique circumstances — with one foot in law and another in science and public health — would lead her to becoming a fierce legal hero for immigrants in the age of Trump.

Scott's immigration activism began when she enrolled at the University of Washington for grad school. There, she pursued a law degree and a Master's in Public Health concurrently — a unique pairing that confused friends, family, and traditional legal employers.

But Scott was confident of her purpose. As her program applied a legal lens to her long-time passion for public health, she realized that immigration was a pressing issue right at this intersection.

In her third year of law school, she worked at an immigrant and refugee advocacy clinic through Northwest Justice Project. The experience expanded her thinking on the scope of what could be done with a law degree.

At the clinic, Scott was assigned to help represent a teenage immigrant girl who had been married off at a young age in her home country, and then brought to the United States. For nine months, Scott built a relationship with the teenager and worked for her safety and freedom. Together with her mentor from Northwest Justice Project, Scott worked with the US Attorney's Office on prosecution of the teenager's oppressors, and helped get her placed with a loving foster family who adopted her.

That case was a turning point for Scott; it's when it really clicked for her just how much immigration is an issue of public health and health policy.

By 2016, Scott had graduated from law school and was practicing as associate general counsel for a bioscience research organization. And as she watched the 2016 presidential election results with her mother-in-law in her home in Seattle, she was shocked and saddened by its outcome.

Over the course of the next few days, she found herself preoccupied with what Donald Trump's presidency could mean for the existence of vital federal programs she supported — particularly those that protected scientific research, public health, and immigrants.

But Scott didn't wallow long in fear and cynicism. She knew she had to shake off the gloom and step up to the challenges ahead.

She started by donating regularly to the ACLU and other

organizations fighting for justice. And when Trump's travel ban was suddenly put into place in 2017, and the family separations broke in the news in 2018, Scott began feeling a strong pull toward activism.

Donating was no longer enough, she says. She searched for organizations that aligned with the issues she was most passionate about. She took a long-term pro bono case with Northwest Immigrant Rights Project for a mom and her kids. Shortly thereafter she became involved with Washington Immigrant Defense Network (WIDEN), a nonprofit that provides legal support to immigrants.

"I needed to make some real changes in how I was going to approach this in order to feel like I could continue to live with myself," she says.

Scott entered into her work with WIDEN with trepidation. Because she wasn't an immigration lawyer, she worried about making a mistake that would alter the outcome of these cases — some of which could mean life or death. But the way WIDEN is structured, with non-immigration lawyer volunteers working directly with experienced immigration lawyers, gave her the confidence she needed to dive in.

What she loves about WIDEN, she says, is that there's an infrastructure where someone without immigration experience can easily plug in and feel useful. They can do research, and write a first draft of a brief around that research.

And while she still worried about screwing up, she says, "The alternative is that these people go unrepresented. That's unacceptable."

Scott still recalls her first case with WIDEN.

Her cohort had been assigned the case of a woman from Central America who had suffered horrific experiences in her home country and fled to the United States. She was apprehended by US Immigration and Customs Enforcement and put into a federal detention center, where she had been living for several months.

The rise in the numbers of Central Americans seeking refuge — most of whom are fleeing human rights violations and political violence in Guatemala, El Salvador and Honduras — is a global issue. In fact, in 2019 the UN Refugee Agency reported 470,000 refugees and asylum seekers from these countries worldwide — a large percentage of them women and children.[1]

And the number of Central American immigrants attempting to enter the US from Mexico has risen dramatically over the last 15 years, according to PEW Research. As the numbers continued to swell in the last part of the last decade, the Trump administration passed several immigration policies specifically designed to bar displaced Central Americans from entering the US, detain them indefinitely, and strip them of their asylum privileges.[23]

That's where the work of WIDEN lawyers comes in.

Scott and her team were called to meet their client, a small woman wearing wet prison scrubs she had hastily washed in the sink. Scott remembers how desperately the woman wanted to be clean and presentable, and how dirty the environment in the detention center was.

The woman couldn't read or write in her native language. Without WIDEN, she would have had to argue her case — despite cultural and language barriers — on her own.

Over the course of months, Scott and the WIDEN team listened to every detail of the woman's story, painstakingly reviewing and re-reviewing with her the horrific events that prompted her flight to the U.S, as well as many other traumatic moments in her life that might prove relevant to her case.

Scott and the team had high hopes that a low cash bond would be granted for their client, since such bond had been set in other similar cases. It wasn't, due to the wild inconsistencies in bond practices in immigration court, forcing the case into a full trial in immigration court.[4]

In that session, Scott was astounded by the lack of empathy for her client's cultural differences and educational level, and the shoddiness of the due process provided overall.

In the end, this detainee's case was denied and she was given five minutes to decide if she would appeal — a process that may leave her in detention for years — or return to an unsafe situation in her home country.

Through heartbreaking sobs, she ultimately decided she could not bear to stay in jail longer and would give up her right to an appeal.

For detainees without representation, Scott says there's a feeling of erasure — and it's not hard to understand why. Detained immigrants are 11 times more likely to pursue relief if they have legal counsel, and twice as likely to obtain that relief than those without legal representation.[5]

So, even though this was not the outcome they had hoped for, Scott knows the importance of advocating at her client's side, even in a system designed to deny a remedy. They were also able to coordinate with the woman's family back in her home country to try to facilitate safer housing options for her when she returned.

The loss in that case motivated Scott to continue her involvement with WIDEN and broaden her view of what volunteer lawyers could do to help refugees targeted by the racist and xenophobic policies of the Trump administration. In fall 2019, Scott and her mom decided to answer a call for volunteer lawyers in south Texas to see what they could do to help advocate for immigrants right at the border.

Just a week before their trip, Trump implemented his Migrant Protection Protocols (MPP), also known as the "Remain in Mexico" program. The policy grants US border patrol guards the right to return asylum seekers to Mexico to await their day in US immigration court. The policy almost immediately resulted in thousands of migrants living outdoors in cramped, unsanitary refugee camps in Mexican border cities well known for rampant kidnappings, rape, and torture.

"MPP is continued persecution of the persecuted," Scott says.

As a result of this policy's implementation, the organizations that Scott and her mother had planned to volunteer for on the American side saw a sudden plummet in demand, as immigrants were no longer able to enter the US and access their services. Once they arrived in Brownsville, Texas, and connected with local organizations, it became clear they needed to cross into Mexico. Good thing they'd brought their passports.

Driving across the border was now prohibited, so the two women covered the distance by foot, carrying supplies for the refugees — including food, medicine, toilet paper, water and other basics – in the baking sun.

Their destination was one of the biggest refugee camps at the southern border, along the Rio Grande River in Matamoros, Mexico. In partnership with the local organizations at the border, they spent their time visiting with and distributing supplies to as many of the roughly 2,000 refugees living there as they could.

Scott also helped a local immigration lawyer by interviewing asylum-seekers and preparing documentation and translations during her visit.

Like her first WIDEN case, Scott's experiences at the border are never far from her mind as she considers the role she can play in response to the Trump administration's immigration policies, and their unrelenting assault on human rights.

These experiences have resulted in a personal transformation.

"I used to think, 'Well, I've got a full-time job, and a family and I make donations and I try to speak out where I can,'" she reflects. "But now I see how flawed that thinking was."

She credits the immigrants she has met in her work — and the activists in immigration and civil rights circles who have been doing this work for decades — with transforming her vision of what she can do.

Because of them, she now expects herself to learn about and show up on issues of social justice in a deliberate way.

"By throwing aside my defense mechanisms and bearing

witness at the border with vulnerability and love, I have tapped into new conduits of energy flowing beneath the surface of my day-to-day existence," Scott wrote in an article about her time at the border.[6] "Their stories have created a spaciousness in my heart that allows me to slough off my old excuses and instead turn my passive empathy into small but tangible action."

SEVEN

Erin Albanese - Business law as a bedrock for activism

S eattle-based attorney Erin Albanese had never considered uniting activism with her profession as a corporate and business lawyer. Then, Donald Trump was elected president.

As the votes rolled in on that unforgettable November evening in 2016, she sat restlessly on her couch at home, watching the television. When the final tally revealed Trump had won, Albanese began to mentally prepare herself for the carnage of such a presidency, one she anticipated would be detrimental for the environment, women, children, immigrants, LGBTQ people, Muslims, and people of color. Like so many around the country, she was in disbelief.

But Albanese also knew that she couldn't remain in that state for very long.

Almost immediately she began to consider everything she could bring to the table as a lawyer and long-time advocate for children. She needed to find a way to push back against the looming impacts of Donald Trump's proposed policies on a range of issues — but especially immigration.

As a presidential candidate, Trump had not hidden his disdain for immigrants and had regaled his followers with repeated promises of a "big, beautiful wall" along the US Mexico border — one that he would get Mexico to pay for.

It seemed clear to Albanese the work that lay ahead. And within a year, she had transformed herself into a dedicated activist, with an integral role in two vital networks dedicated to vulnerable immigrants: Washington Immigrant Defense Network and Lawyer Moms Action (formerly known as Lawyer Moms of America).

She began by re-engaging in something that had been a life-long pursuit: learning. Acquiring new knowledge, she knew, was one way to keep her mind sharp and busy. Up to that point, she hadn't known much about activism, but was determined to learn. She was also determined to get herself comfortable in a courtroom, which she never had in the corporate world.

Albanese soon found that her skills as a transactional lawyer had practical application in organizing and activism. By expanding her knowledge and practice to nonprofit law, she could provide pro bono and low bono services to activists about how to get their 501(c)(3) and 501(c)(4) status — helping to empower organizers on the frontlines.

Nonprofit status, she knew, can create huge political sway for organizations. A 501(c)(3), for instance, designates a charitable or educational organization to which contributions are tax-deductible. They include groups like the charitable arms of the ACLU and Planned Parenthood. Even though they are not allowed to participate in elections, they *can* lobby.

In fact, leveraging labor unions and 501(c)(3) charities was a model used by late-20th century liberal activists as part of the postwar theory of legal liberalism.[1] The idea was that federal courts should be the primary place of social reform, and that nonprofits could collaborate on that effort.

But since then, labor unions have weathered sustained attacks from the political right, hemorrhaging members. And public charities have been prevented from making social change due to a widening wealth gap and increased political polarization. By those standards, public charities were even further immobilized when Trump got into office.

For that reason, more social-change organizations are seeking 501(c)(4) status to become "social welfare" groups. While they do not receive federal tax breaks, the US Supreme Court grants them dramatically increased lobbying power and the ability to participate in political campaigns through candidate endorsements and other measures. Consequentially, 501(c)(4) status gives many key Trump resistance groups, such as Onward Together, Our Revolution, Stand Up America, and The Women's March, more political ammunition.

As a nonprofit lawyer, Albanese was already mentoring and assisting activists with nonprofit status and compliance when Trump's crackdown on undocumented immigration began to ramp up.

In March 2017, *The New York Times* quoted then-Secretary of Homeland Security John F. Kelly: "Children would be separated from their parents if the families had been apprehended entering the country illegally 'in order to deter more movement along this terribly dangerous network.'"[2] The following April, this "Zero-Tolerance"policy was officially announced by Attorney General Jeff Sessions.[3] By May 2018, the US government had separated 2,342 children from their parents after crossing the Southern US border.[4] By July 2018, it became clear that conditions in border detention facilities were inhumane for both parents and children.[5]

A former pre-K teacher and a mom herself, Albanese was horrified by news reports of ICE separating families at the borders and leaving children in cages. In fact, outrage among her circle of lawyer mom friends was palpable. She knew they were thinking the same thing she was — imagining what it would feel like to have their own child torn away from them.

Or what their children would be feeling being forcibly separated from them.

"Just the inhumanity and cruelty layered on top of that..." she says, struggling to even complete the thought.

It didn't take long for Albanese and other lawyers to jump into action, setting the stage for the creation of two important legal activism networks. Both emerged from time spent at the "Families Belong Together" rally in SeaTac, Washington, on June 9th, 2018.

Albanese had attended the rally with several friends she had made in a networking Facebook group for lawyer moms, including Tahmina Watson, founding lawyer of the Seattle firm Watson Immigration Law. Though Watson had raised the idea of a nonprofit dedicated to helping asylum seekers at the border, it wasn't until the SeaTac rally that the two began fleshing out the details for Washington Immigrant Defense Network (WIDEN).

Albanese loved the WIDEN model, the idea of training non-immigration lawyers to participate in immigration cases. And when Tahmina expressed unfamiliarity with starting a nonprofit, Albanese was quick to respond, "Well, I'll take care of that piece."

And she did. Today, WIDEN is a registered 501(c)(3) that provides funding and support services for lawyers representing low-income detained immigrants. According to the American Immigration Council (AIC), only 14 percent of detained immigrants acquired legal counsel, compared with two-thirds of those who aren't detained.

In response to this disparity, WIDEN works with attorneys who specialize in immigration, while also training lawyers in other specialties who want to ensure detained immigrants have access to quality legal representation. As of August 2020, WIDEN has provided in-depth immigration law training to approximately 150 non-immigration lawyers in Washington, and won 50 percent of their detainee cases.

Simultaneously, Albanese was looking for other ways to help migrant and asylum-seeking families impacted by Trump's border policies. Inspired and energized by the events of that June

"Families Belong Together" rally, she and four other lawyer moms — Tovah Ross Kopan, Natalie Roisman, Elizabeth Gray Nuñez, and Laura Latta — formed another Facebook group called Lawyer Moms of America. The organization eventually evolved into two popular nonprofit organizations: Lawyer Moms Action, a 501(c)(4) advocacy organization; and Lawyer Moms Foundation, a 501(c)(3) charitable nonprofit, which has raised well over $100,000 to provide legal services and aid for vulnerable families.[6]

Lawyer Moms Action is a huge coalition, with supporters across all 50 states. It is open to anyone who wants to advocate for the legal rights of marginalized people in areas of immigration, food security, clean water, and mass incarceration. Each chapter is dedicated to sharing opportunities to engage in advocacy with government officials, in educating others in local and national law and policy, spotlighting lawyer activists on the front lines, and further connecting members with the movement to protect families.

In 2018, more than 11,000 people signed an open letter the group wrote to members of Congress demanding an end to family-separation and detention. It was hand-delivered to the district offices of 330 members of Congress by Lawyer Mom members across 49 states.

Now with a membership of over 15,000, Lawyer Moms Action been able to pool skills to create databases, build websites, and directly pay fines for migrants and asylum seekers. Most impressively, they've accumulated over 5 million airline miles, and used just over half of those — about 3 million miles — to fly people released from detention to connect with family, friends, or people who have agreed to host them. Albanese handled the flight arrangements personally, often staying up late at night to ensure travelers made it safely to their destinations.

Recently, Lawyer Moms Action has broadened its focus to include many other issues affecting families — including

COVID-19 — which is disproportionately impacting Latinx people as well as undocumented immigrants.

Albanese says there are so many issues that affect children and families in the US, particularly under this administration, and she wants people to care about them all. To care about everyone in detention. To care about mass incarceration. To care about the prison industrial complex. In this way, the tools of advocacy Albanese and Legal Moms Action have developed for immigrant families — like letter writing, lobbying, and legal education — can apply much more broadly.

The organization's diversified focus is also a reflection of a change within Albanese herself, who has now fully embraced her role as an activist and defender of democracy, and is eagerly looking for new ways to apply her legal insight.

In hindsight, she says the lawyer she is today feels similar to the person she was in theater school three decades ago — more radical, playing folk songs in coffeehouses, and attending Food-Not-Guns meetings. As she transitioned into law school and her legal career, her all-consuming work life began to overshadow her civic participation — without her even noticing.

That history — and the fact that she has found her way back to activism all these years later — gives her the satisfying feeling of coming full circle. It also emboldens her to continue to build on her activism and share her winding path to politics with others in law.

For any legal professionals who want to begin to connect their urge toward activism with their legal careers, she emphasizes keeping it simple and noticing what issues make you passionate, just as she did. She also asks lawyers to stay open-minded about how they might apply their skills outside of their traditional practice area.

"Find an organization that is focused on an issue that you care about, show up, and be willing to do whatever," she says. "Even if you're not directly using your legal skills."

That can be as simple as voting and helping to protect other people's right to vote, especially right now, when so many Constitutionally-protected rights seem to be under assault by the Trump administration.

Currently, Albanese and Lawyer Moms have been especially focused on the 2020 presidential election, unafraid to dive in and do work outside of the legal arena. They've been setting up voter-registration drives in high schools and helping get young people excited about voting — some for the first time.

Clearly, this legal hero is dead-set on doing everything she can to prevent a repeat of that dreadful evening four years ago, and of installing values of justice and democracy back into the United States.

EIGHT

Drew Caputo - The Earth's own litigator

A s vice president of litigation for lands, wildlife, and oceans at Earthjustice, Drew Caputo has a brief almost as big as the outdoors.

He leads the organization's legal work to protect our nation's public lands, wild places, species, and habitats.

And Caputo has chalked up some impressive wins in his day: protections for Pacific rockfish that led to population increases for the overfished species, pulling back leases for oil and gas extraction off the California coast, and ending a permit type that was the single largest means of wetlands destruction.

Caputo grew up in a New Jersey town just outside Philadelphia. He first became interested in the law because of the civil rights movement — in particular, the anti-segregation work of Thurgood Marshall and Constance Baker Motley made a big impression.

"The lesson I took from that," he says, "was that you could use the law to make America and the world a better and more just place. That drove me toward the law."

The most obvious career path for Caputo's cohort at Yale Law School in the late 1980s was corporate law. A high salary at a big-city firm. But working in the public interest was what appealed to him. He was interested in civil rights and civil liberties, the labor movement, and environmental protection.

The summer after his first year of law school, Caputo got a job with the Sierra Club Legal Defense Fund at their Denver Office. He loved the fact that after spending the week on legal work, he could go up into the Rocky Mountains during the weekend to hike and camp in the very places he'd been trying to save during the week.

"That was it for me," he says. "When I graduated from law school, I went straight into public-interest environmental work."

His first job out of law school was working for the Sierra Club Legal Defense Fund (which changed its name to Earthjustice in the mid-1990s). After three years, he moved to the Natural Resources Defense Council, another public-interest environmental organization, where he worked for 13 years, before making the leap to become a federal prosecutor. In his eight years in that role he went after public corruption, national security, and civil rights criminal cases.

Then six years ago, his journey came full circle, back to the environmental movement and Earthjustice. It's work that Caputo finds fully engaging. He found out early on that he did his best work when he was passionately committed, and he counsels people coming out of law school to be wary of the gravitational pull of big-money jobs that may not be right for them in the end. Life is too short to spend 10 hours a day doing something you don't believe in.

"I think the most important thing for someone who is deciding what career path to take is to have a really serious conversation with themselves about what's most important to them," he says. "My experience has been that people who pursued jobs that spoke to them, regardless of what the jobs were, have been satisfied with their careers, and really felt like they've made a contribution, whatever that contribution is."

The appeal of law for Caputo is that it can level the playing field.

"It can give a voice to people and things like the environment, like wildlife, that don't have a voice otherwise, and that can't really operate in the political process."

That advocacy for the voiceless was always important — but is even more so now, under the environmental catastrophe that is the Trump administration.

Donald Trump didn't hide his agenda during his 2016 presidential campaign. So even as he sat with his family on election night watching the results, Caputo saw clearly what was at stake.

"I knew right away that we were going to be facing an existential threat to public health and environmental protection from Trump's election," he says. "And that's a completely nonpartisan and nonpolitical view from someone who has been proud to work with both Republicans and Democrats in service of the environment."

Earthjustice is "an equal opportunity litigant," he jokes — they sued the Obama administration plenty of times. But Caputo describes the Trump administration's policies as uniquely damaging.

"They have thrown in entirely with industry interests that achieve private economic gain by harming the environment."

Right after the election, Caputo met with his legal team and they began mapping out a battle strategy. The first order of business was to get as much done for the environment as possible during the last days of the Obama administration.

Then they made a plan for the first 100 days of the Trump administration, and then another plan for the longer term.

"I set up teams of lawyers, even before Trump took office," Caputo says, "to litigate over decisions that we felt confident the Trump administration would take. So, we were able to go to court very quickly, sometimes the same day on some of these decisions, because we had gotten ready to challenge those anti-environmental actions even before the new administration took them."

Earthjustice has about 150 lawyers working on three areas of environmental protection.

One is the climate crisis — using the law and litigation to fight against dirty sources of energy and for clean alternatives. They've filed a series of lawsuits against the Trump administration's efforts to increase oil and gas extraction on public lands and in public waters. They had two wins this past spring, for oil and gas leases on public land in the Rocky Mountain West that were granted without adequate environmental analysis and protections for wildlife.

Another primary goal for Earthjustice is protecting public health through environmental justice work for low-income communities and communities of color — those who are disproportionately affected by pollution. They recently won a case in the United States Supreme Court under the Clean Water Act, dealing with sewage pollution that was being injected into groundwater and traveling from there to the Pacific Ocean.

Then there's the work Caputo's team does protecting wild places and the species that live there. One of the last things President Obama did before leaving office was to sign an executive order to protect most of the Arctic Ocean — about 120 million acres of it — and some important canyon habitat in the Atlantic Ocean from oil and gas development.[1]

President-elect Trump was clearly planning to reverse Obama's action once he got into office. So Caputo set up a legal team that was poised for a rapid response. When Trump signed that executive order in April 2017, three months after taking office, they sued him within a few days.

Caputo and Earthjustice won that lawsuit, *League of Conservation Voters, et al., v. Donald J. Trump, et al., and American Petroleum Institute and State of Alaska,* last year in the federal district court in Alaska.[2] It blocked the Trump administration's effort to expand oil and gas development in the Arctic, the Atlantic, and potentially in the Pacific Ocean.[3]

But the struggle to save the planet from extractive business-as-usual as well as the most destructive presidential administration in history is by necessity ongoing. At the time of writing, Trump and his administration have just announced a new plan to open the Arctic Wildlife Refuge for oil and gas drilling in 2021.[4]

What happens in the Arctic, of course, doesn't only affect the United States. When Caputo talks about the global impact of environmental law, he has no problem with sounding, for the moment, more like a biologist or a philosopher than a lawyer. He sees the world as facing two great crises that are a threat to humankind and all living beings on earth. The first is the climate crisis that is already causing epic scenes of human misery. The second is the crisis of dwindling biodiversity.

"All life on earth is able to live because of other life. We depend on other species, including tiny species like insects, for things like nutrient cycling, and natural pest control, and all sorts of other ecosystem services," he says. "Human beings have so dramatically changed the world that all of that is at risk. So our goal at Earthjustice is to use the power of the law to try and address those problems."

The frustrating thing for Caputo is that we have the knowledge to simultaneously tackle environmental problems *and* create jobs, by moving from dirty sources of energy like oil, gas, and coal to cleaner, greener sources like solar and wind. The nations that are on the forefront of that are not only going to benefit environmentally, they're going to benefit economically, says Caputo. He'd like the United States to get on board.

The well-being of people is clearly as important to Caputo as the well-being of the planet.

"One of the things that I like about the law," he says, "is that it offers some flexible opportunities to contribute and give back. There are lots of important issues out there, from civil rights and civil liberties to the environment, other important issues like poverty and protection, and there are incredibly worthy groups that use the law to make progress on all those things."

For lawyers working in private practice, he says, there are opportunities to give back to the community through meaningful pro bono work. That's especially important now, when the rule of law is at risk, given some of the policies and agendas that are being pursued in America and elsewhere in the world.

Caputo expresses great respect for the citizen activists who have taken to the streets in recent months to protest racist violence and brutality. They remind him of the courageous activists of the civil rights movement — on the streets and in the courts--that drew him to the law in the first place.

"We are seeing how racism is a stain on America. And there are tremendous opportunities for attorneys to stand up against institutionalized and systematic racism. They can do that from a pro bono standpoint, or can orient their careers that way," he says. "Things that we cherish, like democracy and the rule of law, require tending, and defending and supporting."

They say at Earthjustice that "the Earth needs a good lawyer." So do the people living on it. And we have one in Drew Caputo.

NINE

Shelly Garzon - Trial by fire for a malpractice lawyer

O
n the day after Trump's travel ban, Shelly Garzon left the Sea-Tac airport feeling haunted, and helpless.

The sudden order, suspending entry to the US from seven Muslim-majority countries, had created chaos. People were left stranded in airports, separated from families, and worse — forced to return to the dangerous conditions from which they were fleeing in the first place.

Garzon was one of dozens of attorneys who rushed to Sea-Tac in response to the order, hoping to offer her skills as an attorney.

But she'd arrived to a scene of complete disarray. In that moment, she says, all she could do was "bear witness" to the situation at hand.

In spite of her considerable legal experience — clerking in a state appeals court, working at the Washington attorney general's office, as a medical malpractice defense attorney, and then as a specialist at one of the region's top healthcare law firms — she wasn't sure how she could contribute her skills to the immigration crisis where there was clearly so much need.

Immigration law, and its convoluted court system, is a sea of complexity. Like dozens, or maybe hundreds, of other non-immigration attorneys, Garzon felt she had the time and knowledge to help these vulnerable families, but lacked the specific immigration law skills needed to do the work.

All signs were telling Garzon she should steer clear and not get involved. While she wanted desperately to help, she also did not want to be a bother to those already busy and entrenched in this work.

She called around to law firms engaged in this kind of pro bono work to find out if she could help, but was often met by a voice on the other end that confirmed her unease. It would be too hard to get into immigration law at such a tense and critical time, and no one had the time to train someone who was new to the specialty.

As the Trump administration set forth one disturbing immigration policy after another, like the separation of families on the U.S-Mexico border, Garzon says she was starting to grow physically sick. The horror unfolding in her social media feed around the situation on the southern border was becoming too much to bear, deepening the helplessness she was already feeling.

As a mother, it was disturbing to watch as children were separated from their parents, put in cages, and abused under state custody. So many freedoms were in jeopardy, but even knowing where to begin fighting back felt paralyzing.

Then one day, Garzon found the answer in a social media post about a new initiative called Washington Immigrant Defense Network (WIDEN) – which was pairing up lawyers who wanted to help immigrants with immigration lawyers who had the specialized skills and knowledge, but who were overwhelmed by the need.

WIDEN provided Garzon with the training and resources to apply her existing legal expertise to immigration law and the specific challenges coming up in court at the time.

Eventually she got her first client — a family separation case between a mother and son.

She learned as much as she could about the case to assist the experienced immigration attorney she was working with. Garzon's goal was to simplify the workload for that lead attorney; she spent most of her time making calls and finding resources to put together a bond packet.

As she did so, she was floored at how eager the people she contacted were to help, aware that family separation cases like this one were affecting thousands.

"I think I cried every day for two weeks," Garzon says. "Sometimes it was about how sad the situation was, and sometimes it was about how amazingly beautiful the unity, support, and people's generosity were."

While Garzon was no stranger to the world of law, the technical procedures of immigration cases were new and different. There was an adjustment period, a learning curve, and many mistakes.

Even making paper printouts – a seemingly simple task – required a special new process. Instead of being printed on white paper, sometimes documents would have to be printed on blue, and anything being handed over to Immigration and Customs Enforcement needed to be printed on green sheets. One little confusion with the color of paper printouts and the whole case could be in jeopardy.

Garzon remembers an incident when she came in early on a Saturday morning to put together a thick bond packet for an upcoming trial, taking her time to make neat copies. She used a three-hole punch to put everything into a binder, notebook-style. But her mentor, the lead immigration attorney, stopped her. Everything needed to be two-hole punched at the top of the page; otherwise, the whole packet would be rejected.

The episode was funny, in a way. But Garzon also recognized the impacts of such stringent rules. In immigration court, anything, even the number of hole punches in a document, can be grounds to reject a case and create unnecessary hurdles for immigrants who are trying to navigate their way through an already complicated system.

After that first case, Garzon continued to take on more.

Her second and third cases were similar, both with defendants from Cuba. In these cases, the lead immigration attorney took care of client interviews, while Garzon took on the work of preparing briefs, finding experts, and creating "country condition" reports to establish potential danger in the clients' home country. Finding experts and writing declarations were skills she had previously used in her work in healthcare law. She was able to use her existing knowledge to support the experts who were already well-versed in the complexity of immigration court.

It's one thing to watch injustice play out from a distance – whether through news reporting, social media, or entertainment. But Garzon's perspective completely shifted after going to detention centers and watching the way immigration cases played out in real time in immigration court.

Every day, there were some 20 cases on the court docket at the Northwest Detention Center's immigration court in Tacoma, Washington. Only a fraction of those people had lawyers. The constitutional guarantees of legal representation don't apply in immigration court, even though the stakes are sometimes much higher than in criminal courts.

Garzon once watched a whole session where individuals without legal representation all lost their cases, one after another. Too many things were stacked against them, especially without the support of a legal team who could otherwise help them collect the right documents and evidence, and coach them on how to present their own case.

And regardless of whether a defendant was represented by a lawyer, Garzon saw that the odds were not in their favor.

Garzon worked on three cases through WIDEN, all while keeping up with her day job at FAVROS Law, the healthcare law firm. All three were on very short deadlines and needed a lot of very quick work, including finding a pro bono expert and preparing the client's declaration, prepping them for their testimony, making trips to the detention center to help with interviews and documents, and writing briefs.

In 2018, the Washington Defense Trial Lawyers presented Garzon with the Community Leadership Awards for this pro bono work in family reunification.

More than ever before, the work of lawyers has become critical during the Trump administration, Garzon says. Unlike activism that pushes for change, the main work of lawyers in the Trump era, she says, is to uphold and enforce legal rights that already exist, but that are constantly under attack.

With so much at stake right now, in everything including women's rights, LGBTQ rights, racial injustice, and climate change, Garzon's advice to law professionals who want to expand their scope of practice and make a difference is to just dive right in.

There's no need to second-guess and think twice, the way Garzon says she did in the days just after the Travel Ban. It may be easy to convince yourself that your legal skills don't translate over from something like malpractice law, or insurance law, to pressing civil rights issues that are grabbing headlines. But Garzon encourages lawyers not to think about their skills in those limiting terms.

Lawyers already know how to research and write, how to be organized, how to interface with clients, how to meet deadlines, she notes. And they have respect for the court and know how to work within that court system. There may be times when they need to build specific skills or resources; but models like WIDEN are designed to enable just that.

Ultimately, Garzon believes the most important thing is to identify the work that touches your heart.

Find an issue that speaks to you, she says, and "just do it."

TEN

Aneelah Afzali - Trained in law, forged in faith, true to justice

The day after Donald Trump's inauguration, Aneelah Afzali found herself behind a microphone, looking out over a crowd that stretched halfway across the city and totaled over 100,000 people.

As one of four featured speakers at the Seattle Womxn's March, Afzali was on the frontlines of activism at one of its most critical moments.

She'd come a long way, but it was a fitting place for a lawyer-turned-organizer with a strong sense of justice to end up.

Born in Kabul, Afghanistan, Afzali was two years old when her family escaped the invasion by the Soviet Union. Her family lived as refugees in Germany before immigrating to the United States when she was five.

Like other immigrant families, Afzali's parents and older siblings worked multiple jobs to make ends meet, even as the family once again had to adapt to a new environment and new language.

After five years in the Bay Area, her family moved to Portland, Oregon, where they opened a small video store and market, and later another video store. Afzali worked in those stores, as did all of her five siblings. She also translated and helped complete the paperwork to open the family business — even as a middle-schooler!

An avid reader, Afzali had developed a strong command of the English language; yet she struggled to understand the business documents. The legalese seemed foreign, and she committed to one day learning this "new language."

When she was in the seventh grade, she got her first taste of the legal system. Her father had come home one day troubled at how a police officer pulled him over, treated him poorly, and issued a speeding ticket. Her father complained that the ticket seemed based on his racial and ethnic background rather than actual wrongdoing.

Even at her young age, Afzali felt the sting of injustice. Firmly believing in the American ideal of equality under the law, Afzali insisted on disputing the ticket. She convinced her father, and submitted the request for a hearing along with a subpoena for the officer. She was prepared to represent her father at the scheduled hearing too, given his limited English-speaking skills at the time. As they were entering the courthouse on the day of the hearing, she recalls her father wanting to "just pay and go."

But Afzali was persistent, emphasizing that "this is America" and wanting to make the case before the judge.

She never got that chance. When her father's case was called, Afzali stood up to speak for him. The judge looked at the tween in front of him and asked, "Are you a lawyer?" When she said "no," he firmly directed her to sit down. While her hopes of defending her father were dashed, she still scored a win, as the police officer failed to show up, so the ticket was dismissed.

Afzali's interest in the law continued into high school, where she enjoyed legal thrillers, participated in a mock trial competition, played a lawyer in a high school play, and even helped with her sister's divorce case.

Despite this sustained interest in the law, Afzali still never even *imagined* going to law school. College alone seemed a faraway dream, as she was a daughter of immigrants, a former refugee, and a woman of color from a socioeconomically disadvantaged background. She remembers a family member scoffing at her when she was even looking at college catalogues.

The Presidential Scholarship she received from the University of Oregon made her dream possible, allowing her to become the first (but fortunately not the last) in her family to earn a college degree.

During college, Afzali's advocacy on justice issues really developed, and she set the foundation for the work she does today. She was active in addressing racial injustice, gender inequities, and international issues. She also revealed her commitment to coalition building by starting an organization to bring Muslims and Jews together, and participated in a mock negotiation team working on resolving the Palestinian-Israeli conflict.

Yet she still did not consider law school a possibility.

"People who look like me, who came from my background? They didn't go to law school!" she remembers thinking.

It was not until late in her college years, at the urging of her professors, that she finally allowed herself to dream about a degree beyond college. But her disbelief about such an opportunity led her to apply to 18 different law schools. She was accepted into all the schools she applied to except one, and ultimately chose Harvard Law School.

Entering law school, Afzali was interested in international human rights. This was again driven by that strong sense of justice, and the idea that human rights are for everyone, regardless of their station in life or the circumstance of their birth.

In her first year in law school, Afzali joined a fact-finding delegation to Palestine and Israel with the mission to determine how funds from the United States were being used by the State of Israel. She had completed her college honors thesis on the Palestinian/Israeli conflict, and this delegation led by an Israeli-American attorney — and with Jewish and Muslim lawyers from around the country — was eye-opening. She witnessed the daily injustices that Palestinians endure.

She recalls riding in a vehicle that had to use only the "Arab roads" — leaving the "Jewish roads" for Jewish settlers. Because the delegation vehicle had an Arab license plate with an Arab driver, it was subject to delays, handed down from atop a military tank. This apartheid system of roads deeply offended her sense of justice. She also remembers a young old child in Gaza comforting *her* when they heard Israeli bombs landing nearby. Those sounds had become normalized for the Palestinians in Gaza, even the very youngest. These experiences would remain with her, fueling her drive for justice.

Afzali spent the summer after her first year in law school working with Afghan refugees in Pakistan, where she witnessed the devastating consequences of war, and the disproportionate impact on women and children of unjust policies. She remembers the heartbreak she experienced observing, on a daily basis, the desperation of people from her homeland who had been forgotten by most of the world.

But she was also inspired by the strength, courage, and fortitude exhibited by the proud Afghan people.

While that experience furthered Afzali's commitment to justice, it moved her away from international human rights as a career option because she realized she didn't want to be that far away from her immediate family, and that the bureaucracy and inefficiencies of the international NGO system would not suit her Type A personality.

The passage of the Patriot Act a few months later in October 2001, and the anti-Muslim and xenophobic mindset increasing in our country, only reinforced her decision.

After stints at an international law firm in Seattle, a break to travel, and then working at a smaller mid-size law firm where she made partner, she was hired as general counsel to lead the legal department of a growing healthcare technology company.

It was during that time she had a spiritual transformation, rediscovering her faith.

While Afzali was born to Muslim parents and raised with Islamic values, her family (with the exception of her mother) was not particularly religious. Rather, they were "Ramadan Muslims," as she says, observing religious practices in the holy month only.

Afzali chose Islam for herself in college, after a comparative analysis of religion. But as she explains, "I chose Islam with my mind at that time, and it had not really moved my heart."

During Ramadan 2012, she read the entire Quran cover to cover for the first time, inspiring dramatic change in her life.

She realized she had been pouring her "blood, sweat, and tears" into the pursuit of worldly success. While she had broken barriers she never imagined — like obtaining her college degree, a juris doctorate, admission to the bar, making partner in a law firm, and becoming general counsel of a company – such pursuits alone could be as meaningless as chasing Monopoly money if she did not focus on her actual life purpose, passion, and priorities.

That included working to bring about the change she longed to see in the world – especially in the face of so much injustice and the growing divide she was witnessing in our country.

With no specific plan but a firm faith and trust in God, Afzali left her legal career in June 2013 to pursue service and knowledge — two things her faith strongly emphasizes.

She completed a Quran Intensive program, went on the spiritual pilgrimage (hajj) to Mecca, and started volunteering at the mosque she'd been attending (the Muslim Association of Puget Sound, or MAPS, in Redmond). She committed to performing her five daily prayers – even if she had to do so in some challenging situations like on trains, planes, buses, and more. Later, she chose to start wearing the hijab, to visibly and proudly identify herself as a Muslim.

During this time, she also learned more about "the Islamophobia industry," the network of well-funded anti-Muslim hate groups that spread false information, dangerous conspiracy theories, and a hateful narrative about Islam and Muslims. Their goal, she said, is to divide "we, the people" for profit and political gain.

The Islamophobia industry was especially effective in generating anti-Muslim sentiment around 2010. At that time, a collection of influential speakers, politicians, organizations, and funders coalesced around demonizing Muslims, according to The Carter Center.

While broad anti-Muslim sentiment existed before, this network of influencers manufactured a controversy around the proposal of what they called the "Ground Zero mosque," in reality a Muslim-run community center located close to the rebuilt World Trade Center. And the Islamophobia continued unabated from there, becoming a dominant narrative in mainstream media, political discourse, Hollywood, and common parlance.

For Afzali, the demonization of her faith on a regular basis struck her as vicious, unfair, and untrue. And it stood in stark contrast to the beautiful experience of faith that she and her family were living as they increased their religious practice.

Even before Donald Trump began his campaign for president in 2015, the New York real estate investor already had a history of stoking Islamophobia, including using "Muslim" as a pejorative attack on former President Barack Obama. Throughout 2015 and 2016, as Trump's support quickly rose among registered Republicans, his inflammatory anti-Muslim and anti-immigrant rhetoric increased, too. It furthered the already growing rift in our country, and put everyday Muslims – as well as other communities – at risk of physical, emotional, mental, and spiritual harm.

Afzali wanted to do more than just volunteer work to address this growing problem. But by this time, she had used up all her savings from her 10-year career in law and even had to borrow money from her sister. She needed a source of income.

Because she knew the law, she naturally began interviewing for legal positions.

In her mind, however, she had crafted a vision of combating the growing anti-Muslim sentiment through education and engagement, addressing the negative portrayal of Islam and Muslims in mainstream media, and building coalitions across communities to address injustice. She had even picked an appropriate name for this vision: AMEN, or American Muslim Empowerment Network. She believed such an organization would have a significant impact; but she did not believe there was sufficient community support to make such an effort financially viable.

With her vision and passion on one side, and the need for a steady income on the other, she faced a crossroad.

That's when the leadership of MAPS, her mosque, reached out. It was a godsend.

The MAPS leaders understood her vision for AMEN and asked her to create it as part of MAPS, instead of going back into practicing law. It meant institutional support and backing of the largest Islamic center in the Northwest. MAPS-AMEN was created and launched in late November 2016.

This launch could not have come at a more critical time. Just a week earlier, there was a hate-motivated attack on the MAPS sign. And a few weeks later, the temporary replacement sign was defaced as well.

These attacks were part of the increase in bias incidents and hate crimes across the nation after Trump's win. Indeed, according to the *Washington Post*, reported hate crimes increased the day after the election to the highest level of the year. And the Southern Poverty Law Center reported over 1,000 bias incidents around the nation against Muslims, people of color, immigrants, Jews, and LGBTQ people in the first 34 days post-election. It seemed his victory had validated his inflammatory rhetoric on the campaign trail, and given implicit permission to target the at-risk groups that Trump had dehumanized and depicted as enemies.

Afzali says she had seen it coming. She'd anticipated a Trump victory. Still, as she stayed up all night watching the results come in, she still found it "emotionally jarring" that Trump won.

While she hadn't been a strong supporter of the Democratic nominee, Hillary Clinton, she knew a Trump presidency would have grave consequences for many people —particularly Muslims, people of color, and immigrants.

"We've certainly seen those consequences come to light — not only at the state-sponsored level, but also at the individual level," she says.

Anti-Muslim hate crimes, school bullying cases, discrimination in the workplace, and more all increased after the election.

Since stepping into the spotlight at the Seattle Womxn's March in 2017, estimated to be the third largest protest march in US history, Afzali has been leading MAPS-AMEN with the goal of building coalitions to advocate for justice together, while empowering and engaging the American Muslim community. This includes combating Islamophobia and other forms of hate and bigotry through education, advocacy, and relationship building.

"We need multi-faith, multi-racial, multi-ethnic, multi-generational, and multi-lingual *movements* to push our institutions and individuals to do the right thing," she says.

"Islamophobia does not just hurt me as a Muslim, but hurts all of us as Americans and human beings – the same way that 'All Lives Cannot Matter Until Black Lives Matter!'." That's a quote on one of her favorite shirts, and emphasizes her belief that liberation must be collective.

In the four years since the election of Trump, the necessity of that vision of unity and advocacy for justice has been amplified over and over again — from the Muslim Ban, to DACA and detention of migrant children, to the national uprising following George Floyd's murder.

For Afzali, it's been uplifting to watch communities and coalitions build and come together in solidarity against xenophobia, hate and injustice. Because ultimately, she says, "it is up to us, the community, to love and protect each other, even when our institutions and leaders fail us."

While some of the issues — such as systemic racism in the justice system and the detention of migrant children — existed well before Trump took office, Afzali said Trump's public support and embrace of them have spurred many people to action – whether out of broad concern about the erosion of our justice system, or concern for individuals and communities directly harmed by the administration.

"We're seeing people taken aback and shocked that this is something that would happen in our country at the levels that we're seeing," she stated.

While Afzali often calls herself a "recovering attorney," she still very strongly identifies with the legal profession, and emphasizes the power of the law in the hands of good people committed to justice and change.

She believes lawyers have a unique role in fighting against the current injustices — from holding the Seattle Police Department accountable to its Consent Decree to correct bias against people of color, to understanding the bail process and how that affects people in communities of color, to assisting Dreamers with completion of their DACA renewals, to representing those who are detained at borders, denied entry, or facing discrimination based on race or religion.

Afzali is the first to admit that our legal system is far from perfect. But she believes it is still a system that can be – and has been – used to rein in abuses and challenge egregious policies that are an affront to all of us as human beings.

Lawyers, she says, can not only provide direct representation to people, but also offer advice and communicate vital information to those directly impacted, because they understand what is happening in precise terms. They know that same "legalese" that she struggled with as a middle-schooler trying to help her immigrant parents set up a business.

Lawyers who are outraged at society's injustices need to take a stand at a time when hatred and oppression are being normalized and codified through laws, statutes, and social norms, she says. They need to find a place for their activism, whether providing direct representation, volunteering at legal clinics at places like MAPS, or funding organizations that fight injustice.

The resistance needs more foot soldiers who can bring with them whatever background they have, Afzali says. They don't have to walk away from a legal career, as she did. But whatever their passion, there's a role to play.

Ultimately, the impact is more important than intent.

"This is the time for us to show up and be visible, be active, do whatever we can," she says. "This is not the time for sitting on the sidelines, especially as lawyers who are supposed to be advocates for justice."

Personally, Afzali has come full circle, investing wholeheartedly in the pursuit of justice, which has always fueled her.

And as terrible as the current situation may be, she reminds us that it is an amazing time to be alive.

"Never in my lifetime have I felt we have more power or possibility to make a real change in the future soul and direction of our country," she says. "We are writing history with our words and actions, or inactions. Now is the time to act."

ELEVEN

Takao Yamada - Innovating to protect the rule of law

O n the day that Donald Trump was elected, Takao Yamada had the misfortune of being in Arizona.

"I was by myself watching this catastrophe happen, sitting in a hotel room in Phoenix," Yamada says, explaining that he was in the state to help with election protection. "Not a fun night."

"But after, you know, picking myself up off the carpet – literally – I joined a lot of people in feeling a very strong call to service."

Yamada was born in Los Angeles, but grew up in Ann Arbor, Michigan.

"I fall into that category of kids who were opinionated, argumentative, and kind of into politics. And those kids are always told they're supposed to be lawyers. And it kind of becomes a self-fulfilling prophecy," he says. "I love the law. But I don't know that there was anything innate, other than I liked arguing with people."

After law school at Georgetown University, he moved to Seattle, where his parents and in-laws lived. He clerked in the trial court of Judge Mary Yu, who later was named to the Washington State Supreme Court.

Yamada never became a practicing attorney.

After his clerk experience, Yamada couldn't find a position that he wanted. He moved into political consulting work, and then founded a tech startup with a friend, which they eventually sold.

He says a lot of people, including himself, were caught off-guard by the Trump election.

"We were making progress — there were bad things and good things, but we were sort of chugging along. I think the election of Donald Trump was a really catastrophic change in that impression," he says.

But rather than wallowing in the defeat, Yamada took action.

"Things are about to get even worse under this president and I need to be doing whatever is in my capacity to help," he recalls thinking.

He says he took a "fight every day" approach.

"I made a commitment that every day I would do something, even if that one day it was give $5 to the ACLU, give $5 to Planned Parenthood. Doing one small thing every single day as a commitment to making change," he says.

The mindset helped him get ready for when there was a chance for him to take more direct action.

"I had a pretty strong sense that something more concrete and catastrophic would happen very quickly after the president was elected."

And indeed, one week after Trump's inauguration, the president signed the travel ban that affected people coming from seven majority Muslim nations.

News of the ban brought thousands of protesters to Sea-Tac International Airport, and teams of lawyers ready to help people who had been blocked from entering the country because of the ban.

Yamada connected to the injustice personally. His grandfather immigrated to the United States from Japan in 1907, and some of his relatives were imprisoned as a result of President Franklin D. Roosevelt's Executive Order 9066, which incarcerated Japanese Americans on the West Coast during World War II.

Yamada joined the airport protests, along with the lawyers, protesters, and the family and friends of those who were being detained.

Almost immediately, he saw a problem – and a potential solution.

"At airports, there's really no good means of communication for someone who's traveling into this country who might be detained. You're flying internationally, maybe your phone doesn't work," Yamada explains. "You have people waiting for hours and hours before realizing that the person they're waiting for has been detained."

In response, Yamada combined his own tech background, the tech background of other attorneys, and the advice of immigration lawyers, to build AirportLawyer.org.

The site enables travelers to find attorneys at their destination in advance of their travel, or over WiFi on the plane or once in the arrival airport.

The site has a simple form in English, Arabic, and Farsi, and connects travelers with immigration lawyers on the ground.

Yamada's team had the app up within days of the travel ban.

"That caught fire and we ended up in lots of different airports. Somewhere around 30 airports, here in the United States and abroad were using the app and it was because it was simple," he says. "We just needed a way for someone to raise their hand and say, 'I might need help.'"

Three years after that initial travel ban, which was eventually allowed to remain in effect by the US Supreme Court, Yamada still gets about one request a month from a traveler via Airport Lawyer. Travelers and immigrants to the United States still need the help.

"Immigration has certainly only become scarier and more intimidating as time has gone on," he says.

But the travel ban also brought another issue to the surface.

"There was huge interest in the legal community in helping. But clearly on the immigration front, that's a very specialized field of law," Yamada says.

An average contracts attorney, for instance, has special legal knowledge, but not necessarily the specialized knowledge related to immigration law.

"So we had all these lawyers who wanted to help, and we had to give them tasks that didn't take advantage of their knowledge. And that was really frustrating, I think, for everyone involved," he says.

On the flip side, immigration attorneys were burning out with the number and complexity of cases overall, as well as the number of cases they were taking pro bono.

So Yamada and immigration attorney Tahmina Watson teamed up with other legal professionals to create WIDEN, the Washington Immigration Defense Network, which pairs immigration lawyers with other lawyers who can help with various tasks in immigration cases while learning more about the law in that specialty.

"So those attorneys get a real apprenticeship in immigration law, which is going to be the fastest way for them to become helpful," he says. "You are training non-immigration lawyers to have enough competency that they can help the next time there is something as serious and as widespread as a travel ban."

The nonprofit organization also provides a stipend to immigration lawyers for taking on the cases and for mentoring other practitioners.

"So we increase the capacity for specialists, and we create more specialists at the same time. And that really met both of our goals," he says.

Yamada believes that lawyers have been playing an important role in pushing back against the Trump administration, because law itself is under attack.

"The core corruption of the Trump era is there's just no belief in the rule of law," he says. "It's deep and old and classical corruption that says, 'The powerful should have no laws, save power.'"

Legal systems should be a means for people to protect themselves from the abuses of the powerful, he says.

"That's when law is at its best, when it's giving the powerless a structure that says the powerful have to follow the same rules. Lawyers are the people best positioned to help rebuild the rule of law."

Yamada also sees the practice of law as activism.

"The lawyer sitting at their desk drafting documents to help protesters is an activist in the same way that the person in the street is an activist," he says. "It's all part of the structure of fighting to make a better, more just society."

And that kind of activism is about to become more important than ever.

Yamada believes that the integrity of the 2020 vote is under attack, and that lawyers must respond by engaging in election protection.

He cites the example of the primary election in Kentucky, which showed how elections officials would try to manipulate the vote, and how lawyers put a stop to it.

"They tried to close the doors on people waiting in line to vote. And those people protested, they found lawyers, those lawyers found a judge who signed an injunction, and they had to reopen the doors," he says.

Yamada says that it will be important to fight for restoration of the Voting Rights Act and to bolster the right to protest and to free speech.

But he worries that if the 2020 election goes to Trump, there won't be a lot that lawyers can do to fix the damage of a second term.

And even if Trump is voted out, he says he doesn't know if the president and people in his administration will not be held accountable for their actions, because of the political expedience of closing the chapter and moving on.

He believes lawyers can have a role in making sure that justice is served.

"It's not enough to say, 'Let's all go about our business.' It's not enough to just say, 'It's politics,'" he says. "The rule of law has meaning. The laws have meaning. And the people who broke them need to be held to account for that."

TWELVE

Fiona McEntee - A children's book to revive our immigrant pride

A s an attorney, Fiona McEntee helps prospective new Americans navigate a messy immigration system rife with malfunction. And in the era of Donald Trump, it's gotten even messier.

As Trump's fourth year nears its close, America has endured a Muslim Ban, family separations, attempts to dismantle to Deferred Action for Childhood Arrivals (DACA), a border wall built to pander rather than protect, and malicious rule changes meant to bar immigrants' access to essential services. That's just to name a few. Visa denials are up; asylum applications are down. For immigration attorneys and their clients, the last three-and-a-half years have exacted a terrible toll.

But there's also been an upside. The turmoil has brought McEntee into contact with people with wonderfully inspirational stories. Immigration attorneys like her have a front-row seat to struggle and triumph, adversity and success.

As an immigrant from Ireland herself, McEntee is familiar with the narratives about people who seek to make a life for themselves in this country. It's a journey that many Americans will never experience themselves, because their own ancestors made those sacrifices generations ago.

These accounts are even more relevant as elements within the Trump administration work to undermine the national value of embracing immigrants, and to alienate citizens from their own immigrant beginnings.

The immigrant dramas of the past mirror those today, McEntee reasons, and the nation's children have a right to know it.

It's why in 2019, at the height of Trump's nativist rhetoric, McEntee began collecting the stories of some of her most beguiling clients and of friends and family, and collating them into a children's book.

Our American Dream humanizes the kind of people you'd never think would need humanizing in a nation of immigrants — immigrants themselves. In McEntee's view, there just wasn't enough literature working to fill that role.

She opens the book with verse:

In a country so great with mountains so tall,
was born a dream for one and all.
That dream is known throughout the land.
The American Dream, a dream so grand.

It's a feeling that stays with you throughout the work. The stories, uplifting and inspirational, serve as refreshing anecdotes to the harsh reality of Trump's policies around immigration.

Following the election in 2016, McEntee's more optimistic friends and colleagues tried to deliver a sunnier forecast for a Trump presidency.

"Oh, it's not going to be as bad as you think. He's going to put the right people in the right places," McEntee recalls hearing.

"Obviously, we know that that didn't happen."

In the days after Trump's win, the young lawyer shared her election-night horror with the worldwide community. A newspaper in Ireland was casting around for a US resident's take on the implications of a Trump presidency, and McEntee reached out to share her views.

"As I lie awake in bed refreshing the results of my phone, I am tearing up thinking about how I will explain this to [my daughter] Rose in the morning," McEntee told the *Irish Times*.[1] "While she is only three, she understood there was a 'competition' between Hillary Clinton and Donald Trump, and she knew where our vote would go. She also saw him mock the disabled- on television and she asked me a few times what he was doing. How can I explain to her that that man will be our next president?"

McEntee's statement to the Irish paper was her first taste of media advocacy. It was going to be the first of many, she learned.

It soon became clear she'd have no time to prepare for a new lifestyle as a vocal political activist. The new president was only a few days into his term before all those assurances that it '"wouldn't be so bad" crumbled under the sheer weight of Trump's xenophobia. All political diplomacy was dispensed with. And for those who had spent their lives always expecting better from their country, it was the prelude to a spectacular collapse.

In late January, only days after Trump first moved into the White House, thousands of furious attorneys and activists converged on airports across the country in response to his executive order barring certain people from entering the United States. The arbitrary order stranded untold numbers of US-bound people all over the world. It halted all refugee resettlement into the US for 120 days, imposed an indefinite ban on refugees from Syria, and suspended entry of immigrants from the nations of Iraq, Iran, Libya, Somalia, Sudan, Syria, and Yemen for 90 days.[2]

There was no denying the intended target of the ban, all included countries were Muslim-majority nations.

Many of those caught up in this action had some kind of legal status in the US. Many held permanent residency green cards, and had lived in the US for years. Most were merely returning home from traveling abroad.

Trump called the order an act of "extreme vetting," to keep "radical Islamic terrorists" at bay. One of those "potential terrorists" was a 10-month-old child, according to one attorney.[3]

Because most people were not officially detained, they had no real access to any of the hundreds of attorneys swarming the airports. Any information the lawyers had was mostly gathered from relatives and friends wandering the airport and wringing their hands over missing loved ones. Attorneys and supporters did what they could to scrape up information, file briefs, lobby local politicians, and make calls to the Department of Homeland Security. They also grabbed every camera they could to tell this alarming story to the world.

McEntee was one of the first lawyers to reach O'Hare Airport in Chicago, and ended up being the media spokesperson for the group.[4] Together, the attorneys eventually managed to kick up enough national outrage to secure a ruling from a New York federal judge, blocking the travel ban order.[5] McEntee says it was testament to what can be done when an entire community comes together as one to fight bigotry.

In the years since, her work hasn't gotten any easier. Trump was on target to cut legal immigration by 49 percent by the end of fiscal year 2021. Under his oversight, the US Citizenship and Immigration Services, which processes visas and naturalizations, fell into such disarray that about 70 percent of its employees were facing furlough by mid-2020.[6]

The number of different things that can go wrong in a citizenship or visa application is seemingly infinite. A distracted employee could lose any number of valuable parts of your application. A slip of paper confirming that you hadn't overstayed your visa the last time you were in the US could mysteriously vanish and send you scrounging for long-forgotten tickets, paycheck stubs or credit card records proving you were back home by your deadline. No matter who makes the mistake at the application office, however, you can bet it's up to you to fix it.

These are the kinds of needles that McEntee helps people thread at McEntee Law Group, which she operates with her brother, Raymond, handling all types of immigration law.

Her idea for *Our American Dream* emerged during one of her daughter's classroom presentations, when she realized how scant the available literature was highlighting the beauty of the immigrant experience, and struggles her clients were experiencing. She began compiling stories for her book in February, 2019, citing the experiences of artist Yulia Kuznetsova, former Bernie Sanders Press Secretary Belén Sisa and her own sister-in-law, Faith Anderson-McEntee, among others.[78]

The illustrations, brightly rendered by Italian artist Srimalie Bassani, evoke a whimsical style while depicting the lives of teachers, artists and computer programmers who've come to the US for a better life.

Published in 2020 by Mascot Books, "*Our American Dream*" ranked No. 1 in Amazon's category for "children's new releases on tolerance," and No. 1 among "children's new releases on immigration." It hit No. 6 on children's all-time books on immigration.

Writing a book with a good message is just one of many ways to counter the waves of negative rhetoric cultivated and promoted by Trump and his supporters, McEntee says.

But in spite of the book's impact, in McEntee's eyes, lawyering remains a prime tool for addressing the bigotry.

"There's lots of different ways for lawyers to tap into that activism box. It depends really on what you're looking for," she says.

You don't have to be a seasoned professional to make a difference, either, she adds, mentioning acting as a legal observer at protests or helping with bail bond applications. She refers to the National Immigrant Justice Center as a way to get involved in pro bono work.

For Fiona McEntee, working as an immigration lawyer allows her to make an impact, especially during this moment of intersecting crises.

"There's probably never been more opportunities to do this than right now."

THIRTEEN

Joan Tierney - Retired, rejuvenated, and ready to fight

J oan Tierney has always been attracted to the law. But growing up, her role models for lawyers, both inside and outside her family, were all men. It didn't seem like the legal system had a place for her.

Tierney was adamant that she wanted her career to have a positive impact beyond just her own personal world. Learning about the fight for civil rights during the 1960s was formative in inspiring her to choose a career that centered on justice.

Since law didn't feel reachable at the time, she opted for social work instead, getting her MSW at the University of Washington in 1982.

She worked as a perinatal social worker, assisting farmworkers and undocumented immigrants who needed help finding resources to take care of their children. Tierney was a liaison, helping families — and often teen mothers — find and receive the resources they needed, from diapers, bottles, and food to educational opportunities.

Sometimes she would represent her clients in administrative hearings that didn't require formal legal representation. But Tierney was frustrated at the realization that many didn't so much need a social worker as a lawyer who could help win their cases.

Though law may have felt out of reach for her at one point, she overcame that hurdle and attended Seattle University School of Law, graduating in 2001.

Tierney recognized that while law was a good way to make a living, it was also important to her that she find ways to serve the community through pro bono programs, an ethos inculcated through her law program and professors.

Over the next six years, she taught law to paralegal students at Edmonds College, co-directed Seattle University's professional development program, and served as a pro bono attorney in housing justice and Social Security disability cases. During that time, she also worked extensively in the community as a trustee of the King County Bar Association and as a member of the Washington State Bar Diversity Committee.

But she later realized her social work experience in administrative court made her a great fit to be a judge. So, she applied to become an Administrative Law Judge at the Washington State Office of Administrative Hearings, an administrative appeals court where she ruled on cases, including unemployment and wage claims, as well as licensing, for a decade.

In January 2017, just weeks before her retirement, Tierney walked along with thousands of others during the first Womxn's March. She was already thinking constantly about what she could do in the face of the unjust and inhumane policies of the Trump administration.

So, when the Muslim Ban sent airports, asylum seekers, and immigrants into frazzled confusion and panic, she wanted to help. But she realized that she didn't know anything about immigration law — a reckoning many other like-minded lawyers were also facing.

"What are we going to do as lawyers, and how are we going to do our part to make sure that democracy is not destroyed and people's lives are not ruined?" Tierney desperately wondered.

The timing of her retirement helped her see that she was in the perfect position to really make a difference when the country needed lawyers.

Like many other lawyers in this book, WIDEN ended up being the lifeline that connected the skills Tierney already had to the work that desperately needed to be done, while giving her the support she needed to pick up the nuances and processes of immigration law.

Doing research and writing briefs might have felt like a step backward for some judges; same with procuring housing and getting resources to people once they have come out of detention. But Tierney says it is important to put such skills to use rather than sitting on them. Lawyers have so much to share from their professional training and experience that goes beyond courtrooms and filings.

Time is certainly part of the equation, though. After retiring in 2017, Tierney says, "The world just opens up to opportunities to use your time to help other people."

Tierney believes there is room for anyone seeking to bring their legal skills to immigration court. That can take the shape of "lawyer activism," as Tierney calls it. For example, offering one's skills to join a litigation team, putting together a national resource list — the kind of thing one can do from a laptop at the kitchen table.

Then, Tierney says, there is the kind of activism that is more action-oriented, like organizing a protest or encouraging people to vote. Tierney has a passion for walking, so brings her legs and fitness to help support many causes in walk-a-thons and marches. She also writes postcards to send to voters as reminders to engage and cast their ballot.

In this election year, Tierney says mobilizing voters is imperative, and lawyers have a hand to play in combating voter suppression and making sure they know how to register people.

Tierney is adamant that the right to vote not be taken lightly, and she is quick to say that there is much work to be done in terms of eradicating gerrymandering and remedying a government that has made voter suppression a regular state of affairs.

People died for the right to vote, making it all the more important to exercise that constitutional right. Tierney says that even the simple act of people filling out their ballots is a kind of activism in an election year that's this important.

"And to make sure that it's not just us voting for our own interests, but that everyone who wants their voice heard has the opportunity, and they're not thrown off the voter rolls," she adds.

No matter what avenue one might choose, for Tierney it is important that everyone involve themselves somehow. Sitting back and waiting for things to get better is definitely not an option — even for those who are supposed to be enjoying retirement.

Tierney is a shining example of how retired lawyers have found immense purpose in the Trump era.

FOURTEEN

Bob Ferguson - A real-life legal superhero fights back

A week after the presidential inauguration in January 2017, a good portion of the country was still slumped on the sofa in dismay.

But Washington State Attorney General Bob Ferguson was already pulling off a feat of resistance – the first legal challenge to the new administration's travel ban.

Ferguson had been preparing for this moment for months – perhaps a lifetime.

Like so many Americans, his concern was for the nation as a whole. But some of his dismay hit closer to home. Ferguson and his wife are the parents of twins who were eight years old that year, a boy and a girl. Their daughter, Katie, became a Hillary Clinton supporter, sporting campaign buttons and a T-shirt. When she asked her dad if a woman really would become president, he reassured her that Hillary would win.

Then, on election night, things unraveled.

"To try and explain to Katie how that had happened and what that meant — that was hard," says Ferguson.

It was a tough moment for him in his role as a father. But as attorney general, Ferguson could respond to the election results with greater certainty.

"I remember saying, 'Look, if Donald Trump actually does win, the most important political job in the country will be the job of attorney general,'" says Ferguson. He promised supporters that he would work to hold Trump accountable to the rule of law.

In the months before the inauguration, many political commentators speculated that Trump was unlikely to follow through on the threats he'd made against immigrants on the campaign trail. All that stuff about building a wall on the Mexico border and banning immigrants from predominately Muslim countries was showmanship, they said.

But Ferguson was under no illusions. Having underestimated Trump as a candidate, Ferguson decided not to underestimate him as president-elect.

"I reached out to my team and said, you know, we may be taking on an additional role here for the next four years." They immediately began planning how to curtail the abuses the president-elect had promised.

Ferguson told his team that if the Muslim travel ban the president promised was executed, they would begin working on it as a top priority, that very day.

Taking Trump at his word proved wise. The president's order for a Muslim travel ban took effect on Friday evening, January 27. Ferguson and his team sprang into action over the weekend, and put together a complex case to file on Monday morning.

Meanwhile, airports across the country, including Sea-Tac, Washington state's primary international travel hub, were in chaos. Customs and Border Protection was not sharing information about which travelers from the banned countries – war-torn Syria, with its flood of refugees, and Iran, Iraq, Libya, Somalia, Sudan, and Yemen – had already been detained.

On the scene were outraged immigration rights activists and

lawyers fighting to rescue people from the limbo between customs and deportation. Washington's governor was on the scene, as was the port commissioner, two members of Congress, and Seattle's mayor.

But the hero to emerge as an unexpected national figure of resistance from that weekend was Ferguson himself. A federal judge responded to his case with a temporary freeze of the travel ban, and Trump responded with Twitter insults. Other states joined the effort, and more than 100 companies, including tech giants like Apple and Amazon, signed on to a brief supporting the case that the ban presented harm to business and Washington's economy. A panel of three judges for the Ninth Circuit Court of Appeals unanimously upheld the trial court's temporary restraining order blocking President Trump's travel ban from taking effect. In order to do so, the panel had to find Ferguson's lawsuit likely to succeed. The Trump administration dropped its appeal to the US Supreme Court, allowing Ferguson's victory to stand. The Trump administration even paid Ferguson's court costs.

Washington v. Trump was a bold move by Ferguson, and the first state case filed against the new administration. It illuminated the importance of legal action to defend human rights and civil liberties under the Constitution, and was a model in resisting tyranny that the country badly needed at that hour.

As of this writing, Ferguson has filed nearly 80 lawsuits against the Trump administration; 32 decisions have been issued so far, with 31 wins. That's a pretty good record.

Fictional superheroes often appear in the guise of ordinary, down-to-earth people. Think Clark Kent or Peter Parker.

And in real life, there's Bob Ferguson. There's something reassuringly wholesome and nice-guy-next-door about his haircut, glasses, and thoughtful demeanor.

Ferguson loves sports and the outdoors, keeping score and setting records. In college, he and a friend set out on a road trip to see a baseball game in every major league baseball stadium in the United States. A keen hiker, Ferguson has climbed to the top of the highest peak in 45 of the 50 states.

He's intellectually formidable, a chess master who has won championships and played in international tournaments. Placing sharp focus on strategy and anticipating an opponent's next move is something of a Ferguson superpower by training and natural talent.

Yet when Ferguson speaks in public and to the media about legal cases to defend constitutional rights, he is straightforward and accessible, presenting the facts in a way anyone can understand.

He could not be more different from his most powerful legal adversary, the bombastic, prevaricating president.

Ferguson's upbringing and formative experiences seem to have given him a sense of solidarity with people who are not billionaires — a belief that their rights need to be protected, and that powerful interests that abuse civil liberties and the law should be held to account.

He has deep roots in Washington state, where his family goes back five generations. He grew up in what he describes as a large, "maybe rambunctious" Catholic family of seven children, during the heyday of the Seattle Sonics, when Ferguson's childhood dreams focused on the basketball court rather than the courtroom. It was only after college (he majored in political science at the University of Washington and was elected student body president) that he got a sense of how lawyers can make a difference.

"I decided to spend a year doing service," he says. "I considered the Peace Corps, and ended up joining the Jesuit Volunteer Corps."

He was placed in a low-income community in Portland, Oregon, where he worked in emergency services helping people with food, clothing, shelter, and utility bills, and tutored in an after-school program.

"I noticed that there was a legal clinic in the neighborhood, just literally at the end of the block where I lived," he says. "I remember having the sense that what was going on in that legal clinic was perhaps getting at the more systemic issues in the injustice that community faced."

The idea of the law as a powerful tool to address structural injustice appealed to Ferguson, and he applied to law school while he was living there.

Ferguson says he wasn't sure whether he was going to do that as a public defender or in politics. He followed his interests and what he enjoyed doing, though, and things worked out.

"I want to be helping people," he says. "I just don't have an interest in making money. I have zero relationship to money, for better or worse. I was just really interested in helping people out and using law to do that."

That's a method he advises to young would-be lawyers – and making time to do some work in the public interest.

After receiving his law degree from New York University, Ferguson spent two years as a law clerk for federal judges – a trial court judge in Spokane, then a judge on the Eighth Circuit Court of Appeals. There was valuable experience for a future lawyer in seeing how a court works through the eyes of a judge.

He went on to work as a litigator in private practice at Preston, Gates, and Ellis (now K&L Gates). A lot of his work there was on behalf of public entities like counties, cities, and port districts. And he was part of the legal team that challenged regressive Eyman initiatives in the courts. (Tim Eyman has made a notorious career in Washington state by using the initiative process to put a wrench in the works of progressive legislation.)

Ferguson ran successfully for a King County Council seat in 2003, was re-elected in 2005, and ran unopposed in 2009 – proof of a broad base of approval. Those years of experience led him to think about running for attorney general. The job appealed to him, he says, because it combines the power of the law with an executive position. "You run a large law firm — policy, and politics all in one place."

He was so successful in his first term as attorney general that when he ran a second time in 2016, he won 67 percent of the vote, with no Republican challenger. And in Washington state's August 2020 primary, in a race where three Republicans vied for his job, he won by a wide margin — with almost twice the votes of his closest challenger.

Ferguson often refers to his attorney general role in terms of his duty to the people of Washington – what they think, and whether they are harmed. He's won an important consumer protection lawsuit for the rights of same-sex couples, and a major case against the Grocery Manufacturers Association that violated Washington state campaign finance laws.

About half of the cases his office has led or joined against the Trump administration are about protecting the environment Washingtonians live in. He's met and talked with many Washington state "Dreamers" – people brought to the United States without documentation as children – and is delighted by the recent Supreme Court decision in favor of their right to remain in the country where they grew up. And he points to another important, though under-reported, case recently filed by his office against restrictions imposed by the Education Department under Betsy DeVos about which college students can access financial support under the CARES Act.

Anyone who takes on the injustices of the Trump agenda will be accused of something by Trump's supporters. In Ferguson's case, the accusation is that he takes an activist approach and has "politicized" the office of the attorney general.

But when he sits around the table with his legal team, Ferguson says they're not talking about whether they are outraged by Donald Trump's latest action. They talk about whether the administration has violated the law.

"If I think someone, anyone, is violating the law, and it's

harming Washingtonians, and we have good legal arguments, why would I not file that lawsuit?" Ferguson says. "I really do simply view that as my job. Frankly, if I failed to file a lawsuit like that first Muslim Travel Ban, well, then I would not be doing my job at the most basic level."

FIFTEEN

A call to action

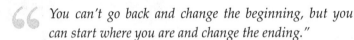 *You can't go back and change the beginning, but you can start where you are and change the ending."*

- C.S. Lewis

The heroes in this book are lawyers like you and me, who decided they needed to do something just a little more than their day-to-day work. There are different lessons to learn from each of them. But there are a few common lessons from across their stories:

First, it's important to stop and recognize what's at stake. Second, you must assess your own means and resources to see what you can actually do to help. Third, prepare your own action plan. You may need to think strategically about the like-minded people you will join, or that you need to convince to join you. Fourth, do not give up on your vision. The steps ahead are unlikely to be easy or quick. And finally, once you have some of the pieces together, start taking action, and keep at it. You don't have to know the precise ending. Just the beginning. Keep moving ahead. If you can protect or touch just one person, it is absolutely worth it.

As lawyers, we're trained to work within the system. We're not advocates for revolution, or destruction of those systems. Most of us are not comfortable being labeled "activists." But what about when those systems are threatened? It is our duty to not just practice law, but to protect it.

Since January 2017, we have seen many attacks on the rule of law. As an immigration lawyer, I have been witness to some of the most outrageous policies in recent history. This administration has simply bypassed Congress time and time again, including creating a series of executive orders each bolder than the next. Since the Chinese Exclusion Act of 1882, we have not had such blatant, prejudiced banning of people coming to the United States.[1] Yet it's now accepted.

We've seen the attorneys general of this administration take asylum cases in their hands to reverse policies that have taken decades to put in place.[2][3] Though the law gives authority to the attorney general for certain actions in immigration law, previous administrations have treated the role as sacred, and allowed the courts and judges to do their jobs. This administration's attorneys general have essentially become a conduit to brazenly changing law in unprecedented ways.

When in history has America deliberately separated babies from their mothers in the name of the law? In the process, international laws and conventions on human rights have been ignored. It is important to be reminded that another resident of the White House, Eleanor Roosevelt, was in fact a central figure in founding the same United Nations Human Rights Convention that is now shirked by this administration. Immigration law is only but one example of the abuse of power by the attorney general and the administration as a whole.

When it comes to our constitutional rights, such as the freedom of speech and right to assembly, we have seen slow but startling curtailment. What happened in Portland, Oregon, this summer was a shock to almost all of us.[4] It was likely the first time America has seen blatant use of unmarked officers and unmarked vehicles to arrest peaceful American protestors. At the time of writing this, unrest in Portland continues.

Trump and his cronies have pushed and ignored the boundaries of the law in so many ways. The American Civil Liberties Union (ACLU) recently filed its 400th case against this administration.[5]

The rule of law is not a vague concept — it is the very mechanics of our society. Each and every one of us is affected if our rights are not afforded via the rule of law. From receiving our mail from the United States Postal Service (USPS), to drinking clean water, to protecting our wildlife and environment, to receiving unemployment benefits when a pandemic brings our jobs to a standstill, the law should serve *all* the people of the country.

One of our most urgent concerns is our basic constitutional right to vote. Not only do we have an extraordinary pandemic causing unimaginable destruction to our way of life and the economy, we have real concerns about whether we will be able to cast our votes, whether they will be properly counted, and whether the will of the people that they express will be respected. The convergence of civil unrest and a pandemic means that voter and election protection have never been more important. In turn, the role of lawyers has never been more essential, as the legal stewards of this fundamental right.

The role of lawyers will also be equally important post-election. Regardless of the outcome, it is widely predicted that we will see further civil unrest. If Trump wins a second term, there is no question that legal boundaries will be pushed further, perhaps even more so than they have over the last three-and-a-half years. If so, we will need lawyers to continue to uphold the rule of law and democracy. And should Biden win, lawyers will need to help rebuild it.

The American Bar Association data states that there are 1.34

million lawyers in America.[6] Thousands have stepped up already, but more will be needed for these unprecedented times that will define the future of our country.[7] Our democracy is at stake, and we have learned over the past few years that democracy is fragile.

Evident from almost all the stories in this book is that the preparation is needed now for what may come between November 2020 and January 2021. This time that we have is precious and we need to put plans in place. Let's learn from what people did in 2016 to prepare. My sincere hope is that as you read these stories, you think about all the work that you may have done, but that you also realize that you can do more. That you can ask your friends to do more. That you can ask your colleagues to do more. In the Resources section that follows, you will find a list of some wonderful organizations in need of lawyers to help advance their causes.

What all of the inspiring legal heroes in the book have said in unison, is that you just have to have a passion, and pick an area of law that calls you.

And regardless of the election, people will continue to need legal help — whether people seek legal assistance when faced with arrests from peaceful protesting, whether people need help obtaining unemployment benefits as the pandemic takes away their income, whether people need to fight for health insurance coverage, or housing rights and protection from eviction, or immigration assistance, or just about any civil right. We lawyers are needed in so many ways.

And for any non-lawyers reading this book, I urge you to find something that you can do as well. We have seen Americans stand up bravely, day in and day out, in support of Black Lives Matter, immigrants, women's rights, LGBTQ and transgender rights, and so much more over the last four years. We cannot stop. All of us need to come together. It's a collaboration, a coalition. It's a movement. And it's an inspiration to ensure that America remains the America that we all love.

If you have found this book to be an enjoyable and inspiring read, I hope you will pass it on to any of your friends inside and outside the legal profession. And I hope that the hero within you and them will be inspired to come out and join the fight for the soul of America.

In the words of Anne Frank, "Everyone has inside them a piece of good news. The good news is you don't know how great you can be! How much you can love! What you can accomplish! And what your potential is."

Afterword - Resources - A Starting Point

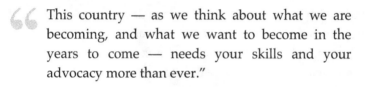 This country — as we think about what we are becoming, and what we want to become in the years to come — needs your skills and your advocacy more than ever."

Julián Castro addressing the 2019 American Immigration Lawyers Association Annual Conference.

Former presidential candidate and Obama era Housing Secretary Julián Castro's words at the AILA annual conference in 2019 stopped me in my tracks.

I was moved by the acknowledgment of the work lawyers had accomplished in the Trump era, as well as by his call to action for leadership from lawyers. His speech articulated exactly how I had been feeling — and in turn that feeling has led to writing this book.

There are so many ways that you can contribute your legal skills, depending on the time that you can spare and the passion that you have.

The way I see it, we need to think of this in timelines:

- From this moment until the election in November.
- From election day to the inauguration day in January 2021.
- And from January 2021 and beyond.

Between now and November 2020, lawyers have a vital role to play in election protection and voter registration issues, and as legal observers at protests, protecting the First Amendment.

Between the pandemic, mail-in votes, and other uncertainties, it's likely that the election results won't be entirely clear for days, or even weeks, after election day. Lawyers need to be on standby to help protect and defend the election results. And it's quite possible civil unrest will continue. If so, the need for legal observers and bail bond assistance may increase.

And regardless of who is in the White House in January 2021, lawyers will be needed — either to assist with upholding the rule of the law in the face of a second Trump term, or in rebuilding democracy and restoring faith in the systems and norms that have been dismantled in his first term.

For lawyers who are thinking about taking action, here are some organizations and areas of law to consider as a starting point:

Lawyers for Good Government

As Traci Love mentions in this book, L4GG has volunteer opportunities around the country, and timely efforts to provide legal assistance in response to the crises of the moment. In September 2020, for example, L4GG rolled out its Lawyers for Racial Justice Initiative. Check out the website: www.lawyersfor-goodgovernment.org.

Election Protection

Election Protection – led by the Lawyers' Committee for Civil

Rights Under Law – is the nation's largest nonpartisan voter protection coalition. https://lawyerscommittee.org/election-protection-volunteer/

Poll Workers

The American Bar Association has created partnerships and opportunities for lawyers to volunteer as election day poll workers under the Poll Worker Esq. initiative.

https://www.americanbar.org/news/abanews/aba-news-archives/2020/08/aba-joins-nass-and-nased-to-mobilize-lawyers-as-poll-workers-for/

Legal Observers at Protests

The National Lawyers Guild provides regular training to participate as legal observers during protests. https://www.nlg.org/legalobservers

Bail Bond Funds

Donate to your local bail bond fund. This is likely going to become increasingly important, particularly if civil unrest continues to escalate in the coming weeks and months. Here is a link to the National Bail Fund Network: https://www.communityjusticeexchange.org/nbfn-directory.

Legal advocacy at criminal hearings including bail hearings

Depending on the bail fund, some may need attorneys to assist with "court watch" programs, or as volunteers to actually show up and post bail. The Bail Fund in Washington state is the NW Community Bail Fund: https://www.nwcombailfund.org/.

Housing Legal Assistance

With people out of work and the economy in crisis, housing insecurity is perhaps the most crucial impact of the pandemic. There is an urgent need for legal assistance to help people stay in their homes, especially as a record number of Americans out of work face eviction. The National Housing Law Project is a good place to start: https://www.nhlp.org/.

If you live in Washington state, the King County Bar Association has an excellent Housing Justice Project, in addition to other pro bono opportunities: https://www.kcba.org/For-Lawyers/Pro-Bono-Services

General Legal Volunteering

You only need to visit the website of your local bar association to find other opportunities to address the great need for access to legal services in our country. The American Bar Association has a lot of opportunities of course www.americanbar.org. And here is the website for Probono.net, which can be a good starting point, too: https://www.probono.net/our-work/

Earn Continuing Legal Education (CLE) Credits with Pro Bono

The Washington State Bar Association has many programs in which one can earn CLE credits, while serving the community pro bono. It's a win-win! https://www.wsba.org/connect-serve/volunteer-opportunities/psp. Check out your own state's bar association website to see if similar opportunities exist (and advocate for them if they don't!).

Special Thanks

A TRIBUTE TO IMMIGRATION LAWYERS

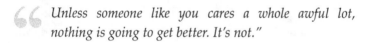

> *Unless someone like you cares a whole awful lot, nothing is going to get better. It's not."*

> — *Dr. Seuss*

The Book Team
This book is derived from a series on my podcast *Tahmina Talks Immigration* **Legal Heroes in the Trump Era**, which was recorded in June 2020. Soon thereafter, I decided that all these interviews must be collated into a book for maximum impact. And thus, the production began in earnest.

A huge thank-you to Lornet Turnbull for getting the project off the ground. To the entire team who helped with so many aspects of the book – Adam Lynch, Valerie Schloredt, Venice Buhian, Kamna Shastri, Alexa Peters, Nicole Lockett, Bryton Tateishi, Leyla Ghesier, Maggie Cuevas, Mim Harrison, and Cameron Doughty. And to Caroline Doughty and Alex Stonehill for bringing the book to completion. Immense gratitude to all.

• • •

My Family and Friends

There are so many people to thank — not just for helping with the book, but for being part of my life, providing love, support, inspiration, and encouragement. As an immigration lawyer, immigrant, and person of color, the last three-and-a-half years have been stressful and exhausting.

First and foremost, I am not sure how I would make it through so much turbulence without my amazing husband, Tom Watson. His steadfast support, and measured and astute observations, grounded my impulsive and passionate outrage. He likely never thought that when he went to law school to become a patent lawyer that he would end up having so much immigration law *talked at* him.

Thank you to my beautiful, loving, and curious daughters Sofia (10) and Sarina (8). Sofia particularly often encourages me and expresses pride in my work. Recently, Sarina told her daddy that she wants to be a lawyer "just like Mommy," even as he incredulously reminded her that Daddy is also a lawyer. These little moments make my heart swell and propel me to do more, particularly because like many mothers, I often suffer from a working mother's guilt of not spending enough time with them.

Talking of mothers, my own mother, Hosne Jahan, is my constant pillar of support, as are my siblings Tamanna and Roman. My mother's example of social work and helping vulnerable women inspired me when I was little, and instilled in me the values to always help others in need. The love and support of my parents-in-law, John and Barbara Watson, has been so important to me. And I cannot tell you how much joy has been brought to me by all the immigration law newspaper cuttings that my adorable 96-year-old grandmother-in-law, Eleanor Stevenson, sends me.

I couldn't do much without the steadfast and unwavering support of Nicole Lockett, senior paralegal and office manager of my law firm. She is smart, funny, intelligent, incredibly wise, and knowledgeable. Beautiful inside and out, she is always volunteering for something. She is a voracious reader and podcast listener who is on top of current news and politics. Being an immigrant to the United States myself, I didn't know much about the US political system. Over the years, Nicole helped me grow in my knowledge and understanding of it. In 2016 she was an ardent Bernie supporter while I was that for Hillary Clinton. And though she practically taught me about the political system, she also knows how to support my views and passions. There have been many times that I returned from a meeting to sheepishly admit that, "I've signed up for something." And while she had every opportunity to despair of my "one more pro bono item," she happily jumped into them all with me to get the job done.

Thank you to my co-founders of WIDEN: Jay Gairson, Takao Yamada, Erin Albanese, and Minda Thorward. They made the vision come true. Thank you also to Jaya Kona and Fiona Dark, our former and current interns. And immense gratitude to AILA WA, Todd Schulte and FWD.us for the generous grants that has enabled WIDEN to get off the ground.

Thank you to my co-founders of Airport Lawyer: Takao Yamada, Greg McLawsen, Joshua Lennon, Ryan McClead, Neota Logics, Clio Technologies, and everyone else on the team.

A huge thank you to the secret Facebook group lawyer mothers that I reference in the book as "LM". Founded by Nina Goldberg, this fierce, brilliant group of women could easily run the world with grace, compassion, and competence (imagine 13,000 Jacinda Aderns!). They were my guiding light in 2017 when the world of immigration was crumbling around me. The sheer fact that I was part of such a powerful group of women gave me courage. And from them emerged the first cohort of WIDEN lawyers who blindly jumped into the unknown of this model.

Thank you to the incredible support I have received on this book journey from Laura Peterson, Allison Melody, Laura

Michelle Powers, Jaime Hawk, Judy Gaul, Jubilee Seth, Melissa Aviram, and many others.

Thank you to everyone at my law firm, especially over the last three years. Without their outstanding, diligent, and excellent work, I wouldn't have been able to do so much for the community. Though some people have moved on, they all played an important part. In addition to Nicole, my thanks to Jacqui Starr, Luka Jurić, Naira Delli-Bovi, Alyssa Ortiz, Taylor Phillips, Trisha Wolf, Isabel Soloaga, and Bryton Tateishi.

It takes a village — whether for your professional or personal life. I am so fortunate to have an incredible one. And for that, I thank my lucky stars every day.

A Tribute to Immigration Lawyers in Washington State

That word "village" took on a deeper meaning when I leaped into action in November 2016 in preparation for what was to come under a Trump administration. And that village, in this case, was the community of immigration lawyers who are members of the Washington Chapter of the American Immigration Lawyers Association (AILA WA).

AILA is a national organization consisting of more than 15,000 members. The Washington state chapter is home to over 550 of them. While Washington state has demonstrated exemplary leadership on the political front, AILA WA has been a shining example of what a group of lawyers can do when their clients and community are under threat.

When I started the Response Committee, little did I know that one day I would be writing a book about it, and I would have the opportunity to express my everlasting gratitude to each person who responded to my pestering requests for help.

Before I list them all, there are a few AILA WA colleagues, friends, and mentors that must be specially recognized. It is important to remember that there was no precedent for the path we took, nor were there any specific roles in place. I was just following my gut instincts. I needed support, encouragement, mentorship, and trust, and Joel Paget and Michele Carney are two fantastic friends who stepped up to provide that.

Joel Paget, a beloved immigration attorney in our community, is a partner at Ryan, Swanson, and Cleveland, PLLC. He could easily have been the inspiration behind the Robert DeNiro character in the movie *The Intern* as he has mentored many lawyers in his illustrious career. I am one of the lucky ones who has had the privilege of his support since I started practicing. I recall many years ago, he waved a copy of the *Puget Sound Business Journal* in which I was mentioned and said I would be famous someday. I don't think writing this book will make me famous, but his trust, encouragement, and belief have certainly been motivating and inspiring. When I started my live radio show (and now podcast) *Tahmina Talks Immigration*, in 2015, I was rather nervous to be live on air. Joel graciously appeared as my inaugural guest, which broke the ice. I haven't stopped interviewing people since. He has supported all my passionate pro bono activities, including WIDEN. His generosity has been profound and I will be eternally thankful for him.

Next, my Response Committee partner-in-goodness, renowned immigration attorney, and former AILA WA chapter chair Michele Carney, partner at Carney & Marchi Law. I learned so much from her gracious and elegant leadership of our chapter during her tenure. She has supported all my efforts and has been very much the wind beneath my wings. Softly spoken and incredibly wise, her advice is always sound, and she brings calmness to my passionate and energized being.

The days following the election, when I was pondering how to get into position to ensure we were ready for inevitable chaos, one night I kept my dear friend and renowned immigration attorney Neha Vyas up until 3 am. Oblivious to her droopy, sleepy eyes, I kept chatting away about what we needed to do and how quickly we needed to do it. Her help was crucial for me starting the Response Committee.

The Response Committee had some of the most brilliant minds of the chapter. One such mind is that of my dear friend and co-founder of WIDEN, Jay Gairson. He is a nationally acclaimed lawyer with a focus on national security laws. When I was flailing on the WIDEN idea, he picked me up, kept running, and helped me get to the finish line.

Bonnie Stern Wasser is also someone for whom I am grateful. While running her own practice, she dedicated endless hours to the role of AILA WA chapter chair for multiple years in a row. And since then, while still running her practice, she is also policy counsel at one of the leading immigrant advocacy organizations in the nation. Her kind words of wisdom have been a source of encouragement and guidance.

Melissa Campos is a renowned removal defense attorney. I met her the week after the November 2016 election, when we were all trying to accept that we would have a president who might cause mass deportation and other heinous acts. She has played an important advisory role both for the Response Committee and WIDEN.

Thank you to the following immigration lawyers for taking on WIDEN lead roles: Lourdes Fuentes, Bart Parsley, Florian Purganan, Adam Boyd, Luz Metz, Peggy Herrman, Liya Djamilova, and Diego Aranda-Teixeira

And a huge thank-you to each and every non-immigration lawyer who devoted time and energy to learning a complex new area of law under high-pressure circumstances, to represent detained immigrants: Shelly Garzon, Jill Scott, Joan Tierney, Shashi Vijay, Kelly Vomacka, Catherine Vuong, Cassie True-blood, Ashley Greenberg, Paula Emery, Amy Weaver, Hillary Brooke, Sumona Das Gupta, Miriam Korngold, Janet Garrow, Kristina Ash, Laurel Brown, Tanika Padhya, Shana Pavitharam, Gonca Talya West, Phillip Singer, Heather Kelly, and Ronald Suter. And of course, to the 150 lawyers who have registered and trained with WIDEN.

· · ·

Thank you to the Northwest Immigrant Rights Project (NWIRP) for supporting the work of WIDEN from inception, with a special thanks to Jorge Barón, Executive Director, and Bill Schwarz, Pro Bono Coordinator.

My immigration lawyer friends from my monthly lunch group that has been going strong for over 12 years have been a source of immense strength, love, and support: Katrina Zafiro, Sophath Chou, Joanne Ko, Rachel Han Huneryager, Laura Hoffman, Erin Zipfel, and Keaton Whitten.

Since January 2017, AILA WA lawyers have stepped up like never before. Whether to attend the airport during travel bans, or legal clinics, or roundtables to talk policy and advocacy, our chapter has accomplished a lot. During unprecedented and trying times, they made our community a better place. Here is a list of all who volunteered at least once, if not more. A huge thank-you to every single person on this list:

Adam Boyd, Ahoua Kone, Aimee Souza, Alex Baron, Allie Sisson, Alissa Baier, Alycia Moss, Amsale Aberra, Amy M. Royalty, Anca Daian, Andrew T. Chan, Annie Benson, Bart Klein, Bart Parsley, Bonnie Wasser, Breanne Johnson, Brenna Bowman, Cadine Brown, Cameron Pardon, Carin Weinrich, Christopher Helm, Daniel Smith, Danielle Doyle, Danielle E. Rosché, Debbie Smith, Devin Theriot-Orr, Diana Chamberlain, Diana Moller, Diane Butler, Elaine Fordyce, Elisa Ford, Elizabeth Poh, Emily Headings, Emily Reber-Mariniello, Eric Lin, Erin Cipolla, Erin Zipfel, Ester Greenfield, Eulalia Soto, Evangeline Stratton, Faye Lau, Franca Baroni, Gabriel Harrison, Gabrielle Schneck, Grace Huang, Grant Manclark, Greg Hoover, Gretchen Korben-Nice, Guadalupe Cavazos, Guastavo Cueva, Henry Cruz, Iona Miron, Jacob McCoy, Jane O'Sullivan, Janay Farmer, Janet Gwilym, Jaron Goddard, Jay Gairson, Jay Stratton, Jeng-Ya Chen, Jessica Yu, Jill Nedved, Joan Thomas, Joanne Ko, Juliann Bildhauer, Karen Egonis, Karen Gilbert, Karin Tolgu, Katherine Collins, Katherine Rich, Kathy Weber, Katrina Zafiro, Keaton Whitten, Kelly Vomacka, Kelsey Beckner, Kevin Lederman, Kim Khanh, Kristin

Kyrka, Kristen Nilsen, Laura Egan, Lauren Ransford, Lesley Irizarry-Hougan, Lisa Seifert, Liya Djamilova, Lori Walls, Lourdes Fuentes, Madeline Davis, Maarij Nasar, Margaret O'Donnell, Mari Matsumoto, Maria Williams, Maribel Martinez, Marie Higuera, Mark Nerheim, Marsha Mavunkel, Meena Menter, Melissa Campos-Castaneda, Merkys Gomez, Michael Tisocco, Michele Carney, Michele Domingo, Michelle Micetic, Miguel A. Bocanegra, Mike Jacobson, Minal Ghassemieh, Minda Thorward, Miriam Korngold, Nancy Whitehead, Neha Vyas, Nema Koohmaraie, Nick Marchi, Octavian Jumanca, Oksana Bilobran, Pam Cowan, Peter Hill, Paul Gill, Paul Soreff, Qingqing Mao, Rachel Da Silva, Rachel Huneryager, Richard Rawson, Rita Espinosa Arguella, Robert Foley, Robert Gibbs, Robert Pauw, Romina Rafer, Rosario Daza, Russell Pritchett, Ruth Yuan Qi, Sandy Restrepo, Shara Svendon, Shelley Badger-Slama, Sofia Velling, Sophath Chou, Stefania Ramos, Steffani Powell, Stella Dokey, Stephanie Gai, Stephen Bernheim, Stephen Brown, Steve Miller, Sumeer Singla, Sylvia Miller, Tim Warden-Hertz, Thomas Lee, Trisha Wolf, Vicente Barraza, Virginia Urenda, Wendy Hernandez, and Zac Bryant.

Thank You to Immigration Lawyers Nationwide

I want to also acknowledge and commend immigration lawyers around the country who have been on the front lines defending immigrants and immigration laws in the Trump era. There are so many that I couldn't possibly list them all, but you know who you are! The ups and downs and twists and turns navigating the ever-changing immigration policies have been unprecedented. It has taken a toll on every individual. Yet, they continue to zealously represent their clients while advocating against policies that are rooted in hate and cruelty.

And finally, there are many immigration advocacy organizations in Washington state as well as around the country that have worked especially hard over the last few years, including

One America, RAICES, KIND, ALDEA, Al Otro Lado, Northwest Immigrant Rights Project (NWIRP), Colectiva Legal Del Pueblo, The Washington Immigrant Solidarity Network (WAISN), American Civil Liberties Union (ACLU), the American Immigration Council (AIC), and Lawyers for Good Government (L4GG), just to name a few.

I want to specifically acknowledge an organization close to my heart that has been at the forefront of working on immigration issues. And that is the American Immigration Lawyers Association (AILA). Under the leadership of Executive Director Ben Johnson and a stellar board of directors, AILA has worked tirelessly to advocate against and litigate outrageous policies, executive orders, and case denials by this administration, while ensuring members like me have the support and tools that we need for our clients.

It has no doubt been one of the most challenging times for the profession. Immigration lawyers have been warriors, and I commend you all.

Donations from the Book's Proceeds

Portions of the proceeds from this book will be donated to:

Lawyers for Good Government (L4GG), a national nonprofit with a network of more than 125,000 legal advocates and a mission to protect and strengthen democratic institutions, resist abuse of power and corruption, and defend the rights of all those who suffer in the absence of good government. One of its largest programs is Project Corazon, a hybrid in-person and remote program providing legal assistance to asylum seekers at border crossings and in detention centers across the country. Check out www.lawyersforgoodgovernment.org.

The FWD.us Education Fund, a nonprofit organization that believes America's families, communities, and economy thrive when more individuals are able to achieve their full potential. For too long, the broken immigration and criminal justice systems have locked too many people out of the American dream. The FWD.us Education Fund seeks to raise awareness and educate the public and policymakers about policies and programs that work to achieve meaningful reforms. Check out www.fwd.us.

Washington Immigrant Defense Network (WIDEN), which provides funding and support services for lawyers representing indigent detained immigrants to increase the capacity and quality of available legal services. WIDEN works with attorneys who specialize in immigration law, and provides volunteer and training opportunities for non-immigration attorneys who want to help. WIDEN hopes to dramatically increase the range and quality of services provided to detained immigrants. Check out www.widenlaw.org.

Notes

1. My Story - Stepping up in crisis

1. https://www.whitehouse.gov/presidential-actions/executive-order-border-security-immigration-enforcement-improvements/
2. https://www.whitehouse.gov/presidential-actions/executive-order-enhancing-public-safety-interior-united-states/

3. Matt Adams - The unifying fight to protect immigrant rights

1. https://www.nwirp.org/wp-content/uploads/2018/06/Wagafe-ORDER-granting-CLASS-CERTIFICATION-and-denying-MTD.pdf
2. https://www.npr.org/2014/09/28/352290026/how-a-journalist-ended-up-on-a-terror-watch-list
3. https://www.thenation.com/article/archive/chertoff-and-torture/
4. https://www.thenation.com/article/archive/trump-terrorism-travel-watchlist/
5. https://www.nwirp.org/washington-man-illegally-detained-by-border-patrol-at-spokanes-greyhound-bus-station-sues-the-agency-for-damages/
6. https://thehill.com/latino/392522-ap-about-2000-children-separated-from-parents-over-6-weeks
7. https://www.kuow.org/stories/least-60-immigrant-moms-torn-kids-jailed-seatac
8. https://www.nbcnews.com/news/us-news/judge-orders-u-s-reunite-families-stop-border-separations-n886861
9. https://www.lawfareblog.com/government-seeks-dismissal-padilla-v-ice
10. https://www.nwirp.org/federal-appeals-court-rejects-trump-administrations-efforts-to-deny-bond-hearing-to-asylum-seekers/
11. https://www.nwirp.org/federal-appeals-court-upholds-block-on-trump-policy-that-arbitrarily-jails-asylum-seekers/
12. https://cdn.ca9.uscourts.gov/datastore/opinions/2020/03/27/19-35565.pdf

4. Traci Feit Love - A visionary vehicle for legal volunteerism

1. https://www.lawyersforgoodgovernment.org/project-corazon

5. Margaret O'Donnell - Bringing shadowy immigration courts under the lights of the stage

1. https://www.migrationpolicy.org/article/central-americans-and-asylum-policy-reagan-era
2. https://www.migrationpolicy.org/article/central-americans-and-asylum-policy-reagan-era
3. https://casetext.com/analysis/special-rule-cancellation-of-removal-or-suspension-of-deportation-for-abc-class-members-and-certain-eastern-europeans
4. https://chicagomonitor.com/2020/08/the-effects-of-president-trumps-muslim-ban/
5. https://www.whitehouse.gov/presidential-actions/memorandum-excluding-illegal-aliens-apportionment-base-following-2020-census/
6. https://globallawadvocates.com/immigration-in-the-arts/the-detention-lottery-2/
7. https://globallawadvocates.com/immigration-in-the-arts/the-detention-lottery-2/
8. Margaret O'Donnell's plays can be found at NewPlayExchange.org
9. https://www.waisn.org/
10. https://www.nwirp.org/wp-content/uploads/2018/06/Wagafe-ORDER-granting-CLASS-CERTIFICATION-and-denying-MTD.pdf

6. Jill Scott - Of borders, bravery, and bearing witness

1. https://www.unhcr.org/en-us/displacement-in-central-america.html%22%20%5Cl%20%22:~:text=Worldwide,%20there%20are%20now%20around,33%25%20as%20compared%20to%202018.
2. https://www.aljazeera.com/news/2020/07/judge-strikes-trump-border-ban-aimed-central-americans-200701150219373.html
3. https://www.aljazeera.com/news/2019/07/trump-moves-asylum-protections-central-americans-190715131018274.html
4. https://www.seattletimes.com/seattle-news/bonds-set-in-tacoma-for-immigrants-are-among-nations-highest/
5. https://immigrantjustice.org/issues/access-counsel
6. https://www.scarymommy.com/moms-at-the-border/

7. Erin Albanese - Business law as a bedrock for activism

1. https://www.theatlantic.com/ideas/archive/2018/11/501c3-501c4-activists-and-tax-code/576364/
2. https://www.nytimes.com/2018/06/16/us/politics/family-separation-trump.html

3. https://www.npr.org/2018/06/19/621065383/what-we-know-family-separation-and-zero-tolerance-at-the-border
4. https://www.npr.org/2018/06/19/621065383/what-we-know-family-separation-and-zero-tolerance-at-the-border
5. https://www.nbcnews.com/politics/immigration/deported-parents-left-out-cold-trump-admin-reaches-deadline-reunify-n894806
6. https://www.lawyermomsfoundation.org/

8. Drew Caputo - The Earth's own litigator

1. https://www.nytimes.com/2019/03/30/climate/trump-oil-drilling-arctic.html
2. https://earthjustice.org/sites/default/files/files/80%20Order%20granting%20MSJ.pdf
3. https://www.rollingstone.com/politics/politics-features/meet-the-lawyers-beating-back-trumps-reckless-environmental-policies-and-winning-887321/
4. https://www.washingtonpost.com/climate-environment/2020/08/17/trump-drilling-arctic-national-wildlife-refuge-alaska/

12. Fiona McEntee - A children's book to revive our immigrant pride

1. https://www.irishtimes.com/life-and-style/abroad/a-dark-day-for-america-irish-in-us-respond-to-trump-victory-1.2861165
2. https://www.washingtonpost.com/world/national-security/trump-approves-extreme-vetting-of-refugees-promises-priority-for-christians/2017/01/27/007021a2-e4c7-11e6-a547-5fb9411d332c_story.html
3. https://www.nbcchicago.com/news/local/chicago-ohare-airport-refugees-detained-trump-executive-order/22969/
4. https://www.youtube.com/watch?v=ssEHQNIRf44&t=613s
5. https://www.youtube.com/watch?v=ssEHQNIRf44&t=613s
6. https://www.washingtonpost.com/opinions/trump-is-so-set-on-harassing-immigrants-that-his-immigration-agency-needs-a-bailout/2020/06/11/52c2ae06-ac1b-11ea-9063-e69bd6520940_story.html?itid=lk_inline_manual_29%22%20%5Ct%20%22_blank
7. https://www.chicagotribune.com/entertainment/ct-ent-artist-immigration-battle-kogan-sidewalks-0410-story.html
8. https://www.refinery29.com/en-us/2019/05/234035/bernie-sanders-immigration-policy-migrant-children-deaths

15. A call to action

1. https://history.state.gov/milestones/1866-1898/chinese-immigration
2. https://www.nytimes.com/2018/06/11/us/politics/sessions-domestic-violence-asylum.html

Notes

3. https://www.wsj.com/articles/attorney-general-blocks-asylum-applications-based-on-family-ties-11564426812

4. https://www.npr.org/2020/07/17/892277592/federal-officers-use-unmarked-vehicles-to-grab-protesters-in-portland

5. https://www.npr.org/2020/07/17/892277592/federal-officers-use-unmarked-vehicles-to-grab-protesters-in-portland

6. https://www.americanbar.org/news/abanews/aba-news-archives/2018/05/new_aba_data_reveals/#:~:text=May%2011%2C%202018-,New%20A-BA%20data%20reveals%20rise%20in%20num-ber%20of%20U.S.%20lawyers,attorneys%20in%20the%20United%20States.

7. https://www.lawyersforgoodgovernment.org/our-story

About the Author

An Effective, Prolific Champion in Immigration Law

Tahmina Watson, the founder in 2009 of Watson Immigration Law, has distinguished herself as a successful and committed specialist in US immigration law. She has helped hundreds of businesses and families achieve their goals for working and living in the United States.

Nationally recognized in this complex arena of law, Tahmina is herself a US immigrant (and naturalized citizen), having moved to the United States in 2005 from her birthplace in London, UK, where she received her education and initial training in law. As a result, she possesses an understanding and empathy that make her work as much a calling as a career.

Tahmina represents US and multinational companies that need high-skilled workers from other countries, non-US businesses opening offices in this country, startups with founders from other countries, and investors expanding their businesses in the US.

Her work in family immigration has succeeded in uniting many spouses, parents and children so that they can enjoy stable, cohesive family units.

A broad public profile

Tahmina is a member of the bar in New York state and Washington state. She was a practicing barrister in the United

Kingdom before immigrating, and is currently an unregistered member of the bar in England and Wales.

She is a well-known media figure in the immigration field. In the Seattle area, where she and her family live, Tahmina is the host of the popular radio show turned podcast, *Tahmina Talks Immigration*®. She has contributed opinion pieces to numerous publications, including *The Seattle Times*, *YES! Magazine* and *Entrepreneur*.

Nationally, Forbes, Bloomberg and CNN are among the news outlets that frequently tap her for her expertise. Her blog, Watson Immigration Law, reaches a wide audience.

In addition, Tahmina is an adjunct fellow at The Niskanen Center, a Washington, DC, think tank, where she advises on immigration policy issues.

Tahmina is a recipient of the 2020 Puget Sound Business Journal Women of Influence Award.

Volunteerism: a driving force

Tahmina's volunteer work has always been integral to her professional life. She points to the work she did as an undergraduate helping children with special needs as the spark that later led to offering her knowledge of the law to their parents, as they sought educational opportunities for their children.

She led a human rights group in law school and has volunteered with numerous nonprofits since coming to the US.

"Volunteerism is something I have carried deeply throughout my life," Tahmina says. "It's what led me to my current work."

Tahmina is a national spokesperson for the American Immigration Lawyers Association (AILA) and the chair of the Response Committee of the Washington Chapter of AILA. Among her honors, she is a recipient of the 2019 AILA President's Commendation Award.

She is a trustee of the Board of King County Bar Association in Washington, a past president of King County Washington Women Lawyers, and a former board member of both the Asian

Bar Association of Washington and Washington Women Lawyers. She is also a former member of the Mercer Island School District Superintendent's Diversity Advisory Committee.

Tahmina helped found the Washington Immigration Defense Network (WIDEN), which trains lawyers and facilitates legal representation in the immigration courtroom. She is also cofounder of Airport Lawyer, which was created in response to the first travel ban in January 2017.

Of Bangladeshi heritage, Tahmina brings another valuable skill to her immigration work: her biliteracy in Bengali and fluency in both Hindi and Urdu.

Tahmina lives in Seattle, Washington with her husband Tom and her daughters Sofia and Sarina.

Also by Tahmina Watson

The Start Up Visa: Key to Job Growth and Economic Prosperity in America

CPSIA information can be obtained
at www.ICGtesting.com
Printed in the USA
LVHW090345241220
675005LV00008B/1377

9 781735 758503